THE FAILED HIPPIE

STUART THUT

*To Bill and Janet.
In Jesus from Stuart.*

© **Stuart Thut 2023**

All rights reserved, including the right to reproduce this book, or portions thereof in any form. No part of this text may be reproduced, transmitted, downloaded, decompiled, reverse engineered, or stored, in any form or introduced into any information storage and retrieval system, in any form or by any means, whether electronic or mechanical without the express written permission of the author.

Dedicated to the Caring For Life organisation
who through their Love for the needy
have made it easier for me to put my
faith in the Love of Jesus.

Is this story true?

All I can say is that it is truer to say that it is true, than to say that it is not true. I don't actually remember many of the details of my story, for example, the lifts I had down to Dover on the first day of my journey, or my conversations with the drivers.

I have had to blend imagination, incomplete memories and other experiences from different parts of my life to fill in the blanks. Most of my descriptions are however typical of the experiences I had whilst hitch-hiking during the years before my journey to India, as well as during my actual journey to India.

Also the descriptions of me as a character, the way I used to think and act, are close enough to reality to be classed as true.

The major events described on my journey did actually happen, and even some of the more memorable details are valid, if not totally accurate.

Most of the characters in my story are based on real people. While I have used some satirization, most of the people I met did not really need any. Even the more extreme characters were pretty much as described – including myself.

It is because of this that I have decided to refer to my story as an auto-novography. That is a cross between a novel and an autobiography.

Chapter 1

An Auspicious Day

It was January 1st, 1974. The Sixties were not just a memory, for most of us they were still happening. I was 18 years old, so the best part of my adolescence had been spent during the second half of this era of darkness and deformity. I was a true child of the Sixties, and I was certainly terrifyingly dark and ridiculously deformed. Even while I believed I was on the side of the angels, or in my case the ascended gurus, I was nevertheless very, very blind and twisted, in what I later understood to be my moral faculty. What I now call my heart.

It was cold and icy with a sprinkle of snow, dull and cloudy, but not windy. At 7 am I looked out of the lead lattice window of my mother's middle class house, onto our middle class road in the suburbs of Nottingham. I hated the middle classes – or so I thought. After all, what sort of hippie would I be if I didn't hate all things middle class? There was an intensity to this hatred that made it almost sincere, and it wasn't entirely without basis or justification within my then limited experience of life.

Strangely I was never that keen on the Beatles, The Stones yes, John Lennon yes, but somehow the Beatles never really did it for me. To me their music had always had a cynical lilt to it that I wasn't keen on, it always appeared to poke fun at its own subject matter. Even so, their assertion that all a person needs is love, seemed like a self-evident truth to me. Those words echoed faintly somewhere in my subconscious, but I didn't hear them. They echoed faintly somewhere in my subconscious, but I did hear them. Without hearing them I heard them, as is the way with the subconscious.

My rucksack was packed and I felt that tell-tale thrill, I fluttered and flapped in my little coup, my bedroom, I was in one of my 'hit the road' moods. This was no surprise to my long-suffering mother who had seen me disappear again and again on a whim, and then return, also on a whim. She had only the vaguest notion of where I was going, not because I wouldn't tell her, but because I myself had only the vaguest notion of where I was going. She had seen this enough times before: Cornwall, Derbyshire, London, the Lake District, Wales, the Continent, with no indication of how long I'd be away, or where I'd be staying. This situation drew forth much sympathetic crooning from her friends, most of whom were parents themselves.

In my superstitious hippie mind the first of January represented a new start, a new adventure, a new horizon to cross, and the accompanying new discoveries that undoubtedly hid just beyond the planet's rim. I was spiritually primed and ready to go. My mind was revving with optimism, flamboyant with images of expectation, defiant of all caution and good advice – I truly was a hippie in every way that mattered.

A cursory goodbye to my mother and my 12-year-old sister who was sitting sleepily at the breakfast table. I ignored our over-energetic dog Charlie who was vying to join me, and I was gone, free of any ties, jobs, responsibilities, commitments, obligations and required status quotients. This was going to be a big one. How did I know? Because it was the first of January of course!

I walked the first mile to Derby Road. This is an A road that leads to the M1 motorway; almost all my journeys started at the M1. I went past the familiar football fields of the nearby secondary school. I had often exercised our dog there. The fields were crusted with frost and scatterings of light snowdrift. I could only just see someone through the lingering morning mist and hear their piping voice, and see a dancing shadow that looked at first confused, then went stiff and static, then surged forward homing in on its target as if its life depended on it, which of course it did. The morning had a silence about it which no longer occurs in our big cities. The 24 hour culture had not yet arrived and a certain rhythm still existed with regard to human endeavour. Mornings, early mornings, were still silent, lonely places to be, places where you could breathe, not just the cold air, but freedom from the pressure imposed by the boa-constricting eyes of others. I was shy. I didn't like to be looked at. I was an introvert, and I knew full well this was not a good trait for a hippie. I found my surroundings comforting; the familiarity and seclusion of the small sandstone gorge through which the lane passed, the entrance to the school on the right, the housing on the left, then the running track on the right.

At the same time I felt contempt for my own comfortableness. This contempt was a form of self-hatred, and it was the root motivation for much of what I subsequently did. Like so many before me I needed to go out there and face some immense challenge; to, as I saw it, evolve into a person I could respect. So many have gone to war, scaled mountains, explored new lands, just to lay to rest their demons of self-hatred and self-contempt. Normally those who live to tell the tale believe that they have been changed by their experiences, or have proved their gnawing self-doubts to be wrong. Even so there was a part of me in all this that I could like and respect. I was an adventurer and an explorer and I wanted a story worth telling. I wanted to come back with deep treasures of wisdom. For me there was something about life that needed explaining, and I was seeking an answer to this mystery which even seemed to elude definition. I was groping in the dark after something beautiful that suggested itself in everything I saw, in the delicate filigree of life around me, in the vastness of space, in the mystery of consciousness. I could easily cut and injure myself on the sharpness of this reality. Somewhat dangerously I could not see its edges yet; it seemed to me more like a diffuse and distant cloud than a ruby or a diamond or a razor sword that amputates limbs effortlessly.

I was already shivering. I have one of those metabolisms that does not accrue fat, so I would not have made a very good Eskimo. I also had a tendency to do things the difficult way. This could include, however unconsciously, not wrapping up properly against the cold. As a result I was not properly dressed for the freezing weather. My clothing was barely adequate to stave off the eroding chill that was already stalking me across the morning. My jeans, the compulsory garb of any half-cool young person of my era, were warm enough. But travelling light was part of the hippie ethos, and my one pullover, and rather uncool anorak, were not really adequate to the task.

Even though I was a fit young man I still laboured a little under my rucksack. It was too easy to over-pack and negate the delight of travelling light. There was something fragile about the nakedness we sought. The savage with his spiritual staff was not very convincing when faced with the bulldozer of reality, but we were believers in something deeper and higher. The only problem was that in our arrogance and blindness we thought that something was inside ourselves.

Though it nagged at my false conscience I still brought a tent, a sleeping bag, and some of that disgusting stuff that people called money.

The lane that led to Derby Road was only about half a mile long. I got to the end of it, then walked the short distance to the roundabout near the local swimming bath. There was the tang of chlorine in the air, a sharp city smell that always made me think of the colour yellow. I shunned anything that reminded me of industry as, I thought, did foxes, birds and badgers and all the other creatures that dwelt amid branch and root. To me they hid in that secluded forest that I sought for my own soul.

I stood at the turning that led to the M1, my well trained thumb tuned for action. This was definitely going to be a big one. At this time in the morning one or two cars were making an early start. Despite the fact that it was New Year's Day, they were probably commuting to Derby. After about two minutes I heard the whir of a distant engine muffled by the mist, soon to increase into an echoing cacophony of susurrating noise as the vehicle swished by, and once again it withdrew into the muffled silence. The silence became even deeper. Was the mist hissing? Or was that me sighing at my reclaimed quietness? Those first few morning cars represented kick-off. Any earlier and people would have felt threatened by someone hitch-hiking at such a strange hour. Now they were more likely to be feeling curious about where I was heading so early in the morning.

There were all types of people who might stop and give me a lift. Paternal types would want to advise me, generous types would want to make me happy, inquisitive types would ply me with questions, cool types would offer me a joint, and predatory types would try to grope my leg. I wore my long hair like a flag so people could easily see where I fitted into the patchwork quilt of Seventies society. In those days society was still separated out into distinct cliques, cults, gangs and classes. Each of which had its own set of values, beliefs and identifiers. Somebody with long hair was highly unlikely to be a Nazi, and was probably a Communist and/or a Buddhist. Unlike today's scrambled egg world, where a longhair with a beard can also be a muscular gun totting thug trotting along with an automatic weapon with a view to imposing his right-wing aspirations on others.

Another car approaching. I stuck my thumb out – anti climax. It carried on round and hissed off into the distance. Another one, so soon. The city was awakening. Normally there would be a distant rumble as people opened their suburban garages, stamped their feet, clapped their hands, got into their vehicles and turned on the ignition. The second car drifted by, ignoring me. I was a little hurt, a little disappointed, more by the driver's deliberate eyes-forward blindness than by being left standing. I was not expecting to get a lift so soon, but this small subtle action spoke volumes and served to throw a little more fuel on my already contorted hatred of regular society. Normally you only had to wait about half an hour at any one spot provided it had safe stopping and a reasonable flow of outgoing traffic. Drivers did sometimes take pity on you when the traffic was thin, and in the early hours of the morning those who were going on a long journey wanted someone to talk to to help them to stay awake.

Lorry drivers were particularly good for this type of lift. In latter years tachometers, stricter rules and mean bosses started to dismantle what was a traditional and almost beautiful symbiosis between lorry driver and hitch-hiker. All this happened back in the age before microprocessor spies that report back to bosses, whose hands are tied by a straightjacket of legislation that means they in turn have to report drivers if they so much as break wind, or else they themselves will face the legal consequences. There are of course always good reasons for all these rules, and this can be proven with statistics that show that fewer deaths have occurred as a result of a particular check or restriction. The overall effect of this micromanagement, however, is a dampening of things like initiative, creativity, debate and generosity, those things that need freedom to breathe and space to move.

With lorries there was roughly a one in three chance you would get a lift, and it was often a nice long lift. So when I heard the tell-tale rumble of a heavy vehicle I perked up, forgetting the attitude of the last driver. And sure enough, the hiss of heavy duty brakes told me he was about to stop for me. The lack of traffic meant he could pull up right next to me. I unslung my rucksack and reached up to open the door.

A face peered down at me as the driver leaned across to the passenger side. "Where are you off to mate?"

"M1, London," I replied.

"Hop in," he said, and he quickly moved a few maps and magazines off the seat to make room for me.

He was a youngish man, a bit older than me, in his early twenties, stubbly face, strong arms, checked shirt, in many ways a typical lorry driver. I slung my rucksack up, then climbed into the cab after it. The driver looked at me with genuine pleasure as I settled in, then he turned back to the road, released the brake and pulled away. As I have already said, lorry drivers were good for lifts, and they clearly enjoyed having the company. Which makes sense, since their job is normally a very lonely one.

I settled down for a nice long lift in a comfortable, warm, spacious cab, plenty of leg room, with a driver who seemed to have a cheery disposition and looked to be on the brim of plying me with lots of interesting questions, which would in turn feed my spiritual vanity.

I was trying to live a poverty philosophy, living from hand to mouth as the yogis did, travelling like a nomadic monk in the tradition of many a guru before me, since this was how I thought of myself: somehow spiritually ahead of the rest. At the same time, in a somewhat schizophrenic way, I knew and hated my personal weaknesses, yet I was not willing admit them, even to myself.

"Where are you heading?" asked the lorry driver. He seemed to have guessed that London was not my final destination.

"Abroad," I said. This solicited immediate interest.

The age of the package holiday, as we now know them, had not quite dawned. If someone fell into the category of that still well-defined working class, then the chances were they had never been abroad, unless they had been in the armed forces. If so, it was more than likely that they had been to some pretty far-flung places. Today, every man and his dog, and probably even his hamster, have been abroad. In those days you could still get respect points for having travelled, even just to the Continent, especially at such a young age as myself.

In most people's minds the word 'abroad' still had an exotic and adventurous ring to it.

"Yeah? Where?" he asked.
"I don't know yet. South, maybe Africa."

I had a vague plan to hitch-hike to the south of France, then to cross the border into Spain, then go to Gibraltar, then to cross the straits to Morocco. After that I intended to navigate the Sahara desert – that's right, the Sahara desert! Then work my passage, or stow away, on a boat to South America, and finally live in the Amazon. So how was I going to get across the Sahara desert? I would figure that one out when I got there. And yes, I know. South America was not exactly on the hippie trail, but a maverick spirit was an essential part of the hippie ethos, and I had always been more than a little bit contrary in my nature. Everybody else was going to India, so I wanted to do something different.

"How far are you going?" I asked.
"Watford," came the reply. "I'll drop you off at the nearest service station."

That sounded good to me, services were among the best places to be dropped off. They were a source of food as well as that all important warming cup of tea. It was also possible to ask people directly, as they ate and drank in the cafeteria, where they were going. And it was the best place to find lorry drivers, some resting in their lorries and drinking from flasks, some waking up from bunk beds in the back of their cabs, some heartily stuffing themselves with large greasy breakfasts in the smoky drivers' cafeteria, while others just hung their heads over rude looking damaged mugs, fags bleeding away on tabletop ashtrays or threatening to fry yellow-brown forefingers. These cafeterias were always stale smelling places. You could taste the grease in the air mingled with the permanent grey mist that was constantly replenished by men lighting up cigarettes, not to mention the sweaty undertones that tugged a little at your gut when you first went in. People were blissfully oblivious in those days to the notion of secondary smoking, and the things that catering establishments got away with cannot be mentioned in polite society.

A time travelling health and safety officer would have suffered permanent psychological trauma at the things they would have seen and smelt.

In five minutes we were at the M1 junction and skimming down the slip road onto a quiet motorway. The sun was starting to rise, revealing a fresh, frost-strewn landscape. Bit by bit the new warmth dismissed the left-over haze. I felt positive, renewed, optimistic and invigorated, all the things that you are supposed to feel first thing in the morning. I was a jangling cliché. If those feelings could be taken out and made into a screenplay they would certainly have made a very good breakfast cereal advertisement. To be fair though, these were also the cold, shiny reflections that spurred me on to new adventure. A part of me scorned happiness as trivial, but this I could accept. And so a few harsh rays of light got past my shutters and hinted at better things ahead.

One handed the driver lipped a fag into his mouth, then offered me one. I was tempted but I was currently in one of my highly spiritual, holistic, holy, healthy modes, and I knew that nicotine was to me what alcohol is to an alcoholic. One fag and I'd be chain smoking by the end of the week. So being a good yogi, I politely refused his offer. He lit up by leaning on his steering wheel; he only had a box of matches and needed both hands to strike a light. Then he opened his window a slit to suck the smoke out. He drew noisily on the cigarette, held his breath and then exhaled with obvious relish. He might have been somebody who was trying to give up or at least cut down on his habit.

The landscape to either side was becoming a tartan of long industrial shadows and silhouettes, mixed with fields and woodland. A flock of gulls rose from a landfill site on our right. They must have come up the Trent or some other local river to feed on the rubbish. A bulldozer levelling the unsorted waste must have startled them into flight. They would wheel around for a while and soon settle back down amongst the tumbled washing machines, deranged televisions, gaping boots, lacerated sofas, discarded clothes, decaying animals, mangled prams, one eyed dolls, bags of dog faeces, burst tyres and rotting food. As we headed south, the shadows inevitably softened and shortened, the day became clearer. It would be a nice bright one; apart from the cold, it was an ideal day for hitch-hiking.

"So what will you do in Africa then? Are you thinking about going to Morocco?"
"Yes, I might go through Morocco and then work on a boat or something."
"Hot place, Morocco. I don't think I'd fancy it. Lots of drugs in Morocco. A guy I know got some of that, what do you call it? Moroccan gold stuff, you smoke it I think. Wouldn't touch it myself."
"It's not addictive," I replied. "Only stuff like heroin is addictive."
"You ever had that?" he asked me.
"No, I wouldn't go near it. I don't want to become a junkie."

There were only a handful of drugs around in those days. Legally they were divided into two categories, hard and soft. Soft drugs were taken by those who thought of themselves as part of the hippie culture, and these drugs were considered to be non-addictive. They included LSD and marijuana. Both of which could be taken orally, but marijuana was normally smoked.

Hard drugs were considered to be terrifyingly addictive and were taken by junkies, who could be seen as a subset of hippies but were generally regarded, even by the hippies themselves, as very different. They were associated with pathetic and craven addiction that uncontrollably led them into all sorts of crime, depravity and self harm. They usually injected themselves with drugs like morphine and heroin. Hippies tried to steered clear of them whenever possible.

"You from Nottingham?" I asked.
"Yeah. You?"
"Not originally, my family's been there nine years though."
"Which part are you from?" he asked.

This bit was always embarrassing.

"Wollaton," I replied.

And inevitably he responded, "Oh. The posh part then."

I genuinely did not want the conversation to go down this alienating route, so I thrashed around in my mind for ways to shoot down my own balloon.

Unable to find any I changed the subject.

I asked, "Do you ever drive abroad?"

"Nah, just Britain. I've been abroad though, Germany. My dad was in the forces, we lived there for three years."

This would have been part of the occupying presence that Britain kept in Germany after the end of World War Two. Many British troops found themselves stationed there, this man's parents amongst them. He obviously felt he scored a few exotic cred points for this rather unusual history, which of course he did.

I wasn't competing with him. In fact it was probably the self-punishing, self-hating part of me that made me admit, "My parents are German."

"You're German then?"

He half turned towards me, his stubbly jowls slack with surprise.

"No. They emigrated over here after the war. I was born here, so I'm British, and they took on British citizenship."

That precipitated a few moments of silence. He might have been thinking that they were Jewish, which they weren't, or maybe they were from some other persecuted minority, which they weren't.

His curiosity overcame his tact. "What made them move to Britain?"

"I don't know. They said they admired the British."

This was a real non-answer, and gave him more questions than answers, but it was the truth. It didn't make a whole lot of sense to me either, but that was what my parents had told me.

Now having admitted my Germanness, I felt that alienation that I had been trying to avoid. This was typical of me: with my eyes wide open, to walk straight into a trap that I was trying to sidestep.

The traffic, though light, was starting to build up.

"How long to Watford?" I asked.

"Another hour and we'll be there. Do you have a ferry to catch?"

"No, I'll just pay when I get to Dover."

"You've got money then?"

He seemed to have a bit of a handle on the hippie way of doing things, otherwise he would never have asked such a question.

"Yes, a bit," I told him.

I felt slightly superior as I said this. I was breaking with my materialistic past and working towards a new, totally self-controlled me, who had no need for what society could offer, who had no need for comfort and who had no need for anything bodily at all. I was pathetically, in fact comically, far away from attaining such a state, I was a sad deflated clown's balloon. The saddest, most comical part of it all was that I didn't realise how limp and weak I was.

Time rumbled by. Tyres tumbled on the tarmac, squashing, gripping and releasing, all concatenating into one dirty blur. Carrying its own thunder with it, and wantonly spewing black exhaust fumes, the lorry made progress along the wide empty road. Traffic was still fairly light due to the New Year. On Christmas Day you could walk quite safely on the motorway as it was almost deserted. New Year was a bit busier with society straining at the leash to get back to normal work, but still the motorway was quiet. I hoped this wouldn't be too much of a problem when I got to Watford services.

Once again I heard the swish of travel as my metaphorical cape blew in the breeze, and my metaphorical young wings opened wide to catch the wind. I thought about the words of one of my favourite songs by Steppenwolf. I was flying free on the highway and I was looking for adventure in whatever the future threw at me.

I didn't have a motorbike at that time, but in every other way this was certainly my theme tune. I unconsciously tapped out the tune on my jigging knee. The driver had been quieter than I expected. He asked me about my school. I told him we had moved around the country a lot when I was a child, but in my secondary years I had at first gone to grammar school. This caused him to confide in me that he had failed his eleven plus exam, and ended up going to a secondary modern school. He did not seem ashamed when he shared this with me, in fact a note of stalwart pride had crept into his voice. Secondary modern schools, with their practical orientation towards woodwork, metalwork and sport, were almost a badge of honour for people from his background. Aspiration did exist in the working classes but you risked being branded a traitor if you read too many books, so you needed to be fairly sure you would succeed if you were going to go down that road. I then went on to explain that I had gone to boarding school for three years, between the ages of thirteen and sixteen.

This had been at my own request, partly because I hated city life. I was and always have been a spiritual goldfish, needing to gawp at the wonders beyond my ken through an eye as big as the world. I needed the countryside setting that a boarding school would provide. I was also on the hunt for the natural. To me natural was healthy, and the healthy were successful, and the successful got the girl. Even at an early age I was trying to lift myself up by my bootlaces and correct my own inadequacies. I had had three girlfriends since then. All had been attractive. The first was a Catholic, so she had locked me out of the one thing I wanted most – sex. She very sensibly tried to bring me round to realising that there was a lot more to the male-female thing than just sex. Being somewhat dull in these matters, and deliberately blinding myself to truths that caught the corner of my eye, I eventually lost what was probably a stepping stone to a much better life than the one I was about to experience.

My second girlfriend was a lot more in tune with my way of thinking, and so I got what I wanted. She was not as interested in me as I was in her, and what relationship we had was no more than a few one night stands. I was living in Keswick at the time, sleeping rough in a sports hut on a playing field. The field was open to the public to walk their dogs or just stroll and enjoy that wonderful Lake District scenery. The door to this hut was always unlocked so I went in. Finding a couple of painter's legs I hauled an open top canoe up onto them and used this as a cot. It was spring when I moved in and my sleeping bag provided plenty of warmth. After a few months of seeing her on the occasions that she came to Keswick to work, I was delivered a well deserved heartbreak. I caught her kissing with somebody else. My hypocrisy in this matter was horrendous since I considered myself to be a free agent when it came to sex, but for some twisted reason I expected loyalty from her. I remember staggering from the pub so distraught that I could hardly walk, and this was not entirely due to drink.

The third girl I went out with was Romanian. I had met her during a holiday in Romania with my mother and sister. Since Romania was still communist at the time it was not easy to develop such a relationship, as travel was very limited and controlled. Apart from a few letters, things soon fizzled out.

So what was I seeking? Sex, intimacy, spirituality, love, dignity, relationships, popularity, ability, success, identity, respect, purpose? I don't think I really knew which, if any of these, was the prime mover in my life. All of these needs and goals seemed to be like intertwined ivy climbing my tree and sapping it dry. It was often difficult to tell the creepers apart from each other.

Finally we arrived at Watford services. I thanked him and opened the cab door to be greeted by the hiss of air brakes as more large lorries pulled into the car park. This was encouraging; there was obviously a build up of traffic. I climbed down from my high perch, pulled my rucksack behind me and slammed the door. The first thing I wanted after a couple of hours in a lorry was a cup of tea. I went to the public part of the service station thinking I might visit the drivers' cafeteria later to see if I could beg a lift from someone. I pushed the heavy glass door and walked into the foyer.

There were a couple of people playing on a Pong video machine. This represented the pinnacle of technological achievement: a TV screen controlled by a computer. 'Wow!' and double 'Wow!' The word 'computer' sent a small visceral shiver down my lower back. This was evolution! This was hope! Hope of what? Space? New consciousness? Who knew what!

It was thrilling that the dream of such hi-tech was finally manifesting and reaching into the hands of ordinary people. The black and white image of two simple rectangles moving up and down on the screen had caught the interest of a couple of bystanders, and I paused for a second to take it all in. The game made its signature beep, as the 'ball' hit the simple bat and angled off at a presumably correct trajectory across to the other side. Amazing! Where would this take us next?

The constant stale taste of tobacco smoke tainted the air, as it did in all public places. A slight yellowing of every surface, even in this slick, chrome plated, super-tech environment. The subtle greying of the atmosphere belied the fresh aerated image suggested by the big windows pouring in extra sunlight that shafted through a thin smog. I queued, ever conscious of my bohemian image. A part of me was proud of it, but another part, the reclusive introvert, didn't like the attention. I knew I stood out as different in an age where the word 'normal' still had meaning. What I didn't know was how much, in reality, I pined for that normality that I so despised. The queues in these places were always slow, as people slid their trays along towards the till, picking up food and drink along the way. I opted for a pot of tea and checked that I had got all the paraphernalia that was involved: cup, saucer, pot, teabag, water, jug, milk, sugar and teaspoon. Why couldn't they just do mugs of tea like the lorry drivers' café?

I then went to search for an uncomfortably rigid plastic seat, fixed to an uncomfortably rigid plastic table, near a pleasantly bright window, that was as far away from other people as possible. I've always suffered from a mild claustrophobia and naturally gravitate towards open views and spacious places. Since the services were not busy I found my ideal spot quite easily. I sat down with a sigh that had nothing to do with age but a lot to do with state of mind, and unloaded the contents of my tray onto the table, shoving the overstuffed ashtray to one side to make room. The table hadn't been wiped; this irritated me more that I cared to admit. Working between the blobs of – was it coffee? – I sugared my tea and started to sip. I don't know why, but motorway tea never satisfied me, there was always something a bit wrong with the flavour. I persevered knowing it would at least have a stimulating effect, even if it didn't taste so good. Greasy smells of frying coiled themselves into my nostrils; the smoke was hiding demons with sizzling rashers of bacon stuck on the ends of their red hot forks. It was so tempting. I was supposed to be a vegetarian, being such a highly evolved yogi and all that, but my love of all things savoury meant I often lapsed. As there was little else on the morning menu, slapping my thigh amid thunder clouds of self contempt I gave in to my baser instincts. This sort of behaviour I believed dragged me that bit further from detachment from my body, and from that eventual Nirvana that I sought. So having let oneness with the universe get usurped by a full English breakfast, I reassessed my financial situation. I didn't have a great deal of money, the idea was to do it all for free. 'Free' was somehow an operative word in hippie thinking. We were looking for nakedness in all things, nakedness from anxiety and all the other burdens this world had to offer. To us all burdens were bad, even the ones that some people referred to as responsibilities. I had already begged for a living when I lived in the Lake District that previous summer. For someone as sensitive as myself, that was not a good move. Some people were kind and gave, but others just snubbed me. My technique was simply to go up to people and ask for money. In society the whole concept of the hippie beggar was still new and a lot of people hadn't thought it through yet, so they just gave because they didn't know what else to do. I do not believe I was ever threatening, and hope that I was never perceived as such. Today many people do not give to beggars because they believe that they will spend the money on drink, cigarettes and drugs. I certainly spent my money on drink and cigarettes, as well as fish and chips and tea. This did not seem dishonest to me at the time. After all, most people had plenty of money. It was only years later that it occurred to me that I had been taking advantage of other people's generosity.

Having finished the devil's breakfast, and feeling my Yin-Yang balance fall over dead, I contemplated my next move. I needed a lift that got me around to the other side of London, I did not want to be stuck on some busy ring road with no safe stopping spots, and only local drivers who had no idea where I was heading, and at best would give me piecemeal lifts for a few miles down the road. That was one of the classic hitch-hiker's nightmares, inhaling car fumes until they made you feel sick, and listening to the grumble of traffic till it made your ears ring. I decided to ask at a few tables. Leaving my rucksack where I could see it I drifted around, tactfully sauntering up to tables occupied by people and asking if they were going to Dover. I didn't have any luck. Most were polite, one or two were a little abrupt, but nobody was rude. So I picked up my rucksack and went for a quick look at the traffic from the motorway footbridge. Most services had them, so that you could walk to the other side of the motorway and visit the shops or whatever. It was obvious that the volume of traffic on the motorway had picked up. It still wasn't full on, but vehicles were certainly passing under fairly frequently. Since the day had brightened up a bit, and I wanted a change from this sticky, tainted environment, I decided to go outside and try to hitch a lift on the motorway access road. I trotted down the stairs and as I opened the front door the cold fresh air hit me straight away. Picking my way between the parked lorries with a constant sense of my vulnerability amongst these juggernauts, I made my way to the service station exit road. I was glad to see there were no other hitch-hikers there, otherwise I would have had to take up a position downstream from them and wait till they got a lift first. It wasn't the time of year for hitch-hiking; the only people who hitch-hiked on the first of January were intrepid adventurers (nutters) like me and Scotsmen called Jimmy, who were always from Glasgow, and always on the run from the police.

In the first half hour I had been passed up by a couple of lorries and four cars, and then the third lorry stopped. When I asked the driver where he was going, he was only going into London, not around it to the other side, which would have meant I would have had to deal with the complexities of London. It certainly wasn't worth it.

I had brought gloves, but my feet were not adequately shod for cold weather and my toes were starting to feel it. I stamped my feet, jumped up and down, and blew clouds of chill air into my gloves. It was still bright but the sun had misted over a bit, turning pleasant and fresh into frigid and miserable. If I went any further I knew I would be beyond the point of no return as far as getting back home that day was concerned. So whatever the weather dealt me later tonight, I would have to cope. But this was all part of the adventure, not exactly 'Scott of the Antarctic' but close enough for me at this stage of the game.

Despite being a hippie, a lot of the things I was trying to do were very much in line with my old boarding school ethos. I was trying to get myself under control with yoga, so that I was cool and competent in all situations. I was challenging myself with spartan and stressful situations to toughen myself up. This walked happily hand in hand with detaching myself from material needs. In some way I wanted to be a leader, since I wanted to be a deep yogi, or perhaps a warlock if you were thinking in terms of Western occultism. Yet there was tension in me. These two sets of notions, school values and hippie thinking, were in conflict with each other one minute, then confirming each other the next minute. Too often a finger would point at me and I would hear the word 'pseudo – pseudo – pseudo' suggesting there was something fundamental to being a hippie that I had not yet understood, that was still somehow beyond my spiritual grasp. This voice suggested that deep down I was still a toffee-nosed boarding school boy, and told me that in my previous life I had been something very low like a dog or a snake, and that I could not hope for any real spiritual attainment in this life.

As well as Eastern mysticism I also had a belief in Western occultism, though my understanding was muddled. The beliefs themselves seemed to me to be incoherent and contradictory. This did not bother me too much at the time, as I thought it was my lack of grasp on these ideas that made them so confusing. I was determined to learn more. The fact that I was leaning more towards Eastern thinking rather than Western thinking didn't really seem like an inconsistency to me, since I thought it was all just a different form of the same thing.

A car pulled up level with me; my hopes leapt. I opened the passenger door.
The driver leant over. "Where are you heading?" he asked.
"I'm going to Dover. Are you going past London? I don't want to be stuck in London."
"I'm going half way to Dover, if that's any help?"
"That's great, that'll be a lot of help, thanks!".
I got into the passenger seat next to him and in my enthusiasm I pulled my rucksack onto my lap, forgetting how big it was. He suggested that I put in on the back seat. I squeezed and stuffed it through the gap between the front seats, and it landed upside-down on the rear seat.
Then we were off. A wash of relief as I realised the London problem was dealt with, no waiting for hours for bitty five mile hops. Once again I was getting a lift from a youngish male with a pleasant disposition. This guy looked like a professional of some sort. His dress style was smartly

casual, a polo-necked pullover and slacks. He was in fact a solicitor's assistant and had been visiting his fiancée up north.

Marriage was so uncool in my reckoning. I personally was looking for as much casual sex as I could get, which in my case wasn't much, while at the same time looking for that one with whom I could have some sort of meaningful romance. But not forever, just a year or two maybe. In fact I scorned the whole notion of marriage as something that 'straight' people did. The hippie culture used the term 'straight' to refer to anyone who was socially compliant, law abiding, moral or concerned about the status quo. The term was always used derisively. I for one had not made the connection with hard criminality, that is, 'straight' as opposed to 'bent'. I'm not sure how many of us realised that the term probably had its origins in the underworld and in prison society. We considered ourselves to be pacifistic freedom fighters, rebels for the cause, not villains.

We hardly felt London as we passed it. Not being a driver I had no idea what route he took to bypass this complex problem, but it did not seem to be long before we were seeing signs to towns and cities south of London. The vehicle had a car compass stuck to the dashboard. These could be surprisingly useful back in the days when sat-navs only existed in the hands of the most advanced alien monsters, in the most flea-bitten low grade science fiction movies, or in the dark bowels of some top secret missile silo, tasked with some sinister incendiary purpose.

Once again we were on a motorway; from the wobbling compass needle I saw that we were heading in a more easterly direction. The road signs told us we were going towards Sevenoaks and Maidstone. I was surprised to find that it was approaching one o'clock. The weather had darkened and chilled down considerably since leaving the services. At this time of year it would not be long before the sun was setting. There is always a little bit of regret at giving up a warm soft bed when you realise that you will have to cope with a cold night, sleeping on hard lumpy ground. But, as any nomad will tell you, that is all part of the deal; the alternative is to give up your freedom and settle down. 'Settling down' was another 'straight' characteristic, to be avoided if you wanted to be rated as cool in accordance with the hippie status quo manual Section 7 'How to be Cool' Subsection 3.5 'Moving On'.

I asked the driver how much further he was taking me; he told me another hour and he would be turning off. He asked me if I wanted to be dropped off at another services, or on a junction slip road. Given the weather and the time of day I opted for the services. I had noticed large spreads of immature woodland along the side of the motorway, and a vague plan was forming in my mind. I had a small tent, and if I went deep enough into one of these woods I could set up and camp for the night, and my sleeping bag would keep me reasonably warm, or so I thought.

It took us about three quarters of an hour to reach the services. We had had an interesting conversation about UFO's and life on other worlds. We both agreed there had to be life in other worlds, and that UFO's must be just what they seemed to be, that is, alien spacecraft. My beliefs had a more mystical dimension to them though. I believed these aliens were bound to be highly evolved and benign, whereas he entertained the possibility that they were dangerous and in the habit of abducting people for nefarious reasons. He told me about a friend of his sister who believed she had been abducted by aliens, and had spent several years in a mental hospital terrified that they were out to recapture her and stab her full of probes. Apparently she had been the picture of stability and sanity up until that point in time. He did mention that the onset of her illness had coincided with a certain amount of drug experimentation, and that he questioned the validity of her experience as a result.

All this was pretty standard stuff for me. Conversations during lifts often tilted into talk about UFO's or spirituality. Sometimes the conversation was about drugs and morality. On such occasions, if the lift giver was of the older generation they often took the moral high ground and condescended to correct me. Or they might be of the more kindly parental type, concerned for my well-being if I continued down this questionable road. In response I would defend my ridiculously amoral positions, politely pouring vitriolic contempt onto their precious pearls of wisdom.

Many of my views were based to a large extent on the notion of nobody truly owning anything as personal property. Often what we called Red Indians, now known as Native Americans, were held up by hippies as indisputable proof of the virtues of such attitudes towards possessions and relationships. In fact all we hippies saw were their pretty beads and their colourful child-like paintings, along with their closeness to nature. The fact that they had medicine men who mixed herbs and mushrooms and went into strange trances also helped to ingratiate them to us.

While it is true that these peoples often danced in harmony with nature it didn't occur to us that there were in fact many different tribes of Native Americans, most of whom were warlike and wouldn't think twice about knocking seven bells out of their neighbours while raping their wives and enslaving their children.

Chapter 2

Beyond The Haunted Wood

We finally got to the services. I thanked the driver for the lift, closed the door and he drove off. He obviously didn't want to hang about, being so close to home. Neither did I really, it was almost two o'clock and would soon be getting dark. I nipped into the service station to buy some chocolate and some crisps for later, then went straight back out and started hitch-hiking on the service station's exit road. It was gloomy and chilly but not windy. I was there for about three quarters of an hour and was just starting to get a bit discouraged when a car passed me and came to a halt about 20 yards further down the road. It didn't happen often, but some people enjoyed teasing you by pulling up and then driving away as you ran towards them. Thankfully this person was not of that type, he let me in and told me he was going another 40 miles. I accepted the offer. Most lift givers were males. For obvious reasons females were nearly always with someone else if they stopped. This man was older than the other two who had picked me up earlier that day. He was probably in his forties, a little overweight and dressed in tweeds. The car smelt strongly of cigarette smoke and there were bits of ash here and there that hadn't yet entropied into smears through the vibration of the vehicle. I coughed harshly; this was a little residual asthma from childhood and only partly because of the cold from outside. He put a fag in his mouth, lit up, and pulled away. The cigarettes were stinky French ones. Even when I did smoke I would steer clear of these because they always made me feel sick. I opened my window a slit. He didn't seem to mind. He was a school teacher, secondary kids, geography. I told him I had a few O levels but not in geography. He asked me if I had thought of going on to further education. I replied that I had tried an art course at an FE College in Nottingham but it had only lasted a few days before I decided it was not for me. I remember starting it with enthusiasm and excitement, especially since there was a social dimension involved in going to college, but soon my motivation had flopped as I realised this wasn't going to give me the gratification I sought. I cannot say exactly why I felt that way. Maybe it wasn't instantaneous enough, and I saw that it would take work before I was going to be any good at art, or maybe I sensed that however helpful art might be on an emotional level it still would not strike deep enough to fulfil me or to heal me where it counted.

Dusk was setting in. I noticed more of that immature deciduous woodland running along the side of the motorway. "Do you think I could camp in there?" I asked him.

"It's a bit cold for camping isn't it? What sort of tent have you got?"

"Just a small two-person," I replied.

He looked at me side-on with a dubious slant, his spectacles glinting, clearly asking himself *Is this guy unhinged?*

"Could you pull up on the hard shoulder next time we see a decent piece of woodland?" I said.

"Are you sure?" he asked.

"Yes. Nobody will bother me in there and I can hitch-hike from the hard shoulder in the morning."

After about five minutes I saw some trees that looked just right. They extended back deep into the flat distance. If these woods were private then they were too thick and extensive for anyone to patrol effectively. I would not be bothered in there, of that I was fairly confident. I pointed them out to the driver, and he reluctantly pulled over onto the hard shoulder. I got out with my rucksack, gave him the usual ritual 'thank you' and watched him pull away. I turned to assess the fence I'd have to negotiate. It was plain wire and didn't look as if it would present any difficulty. After all, who expected someone to climb in off the motorway?

After clambering through the fence and pulling my rucksack behind me I struck out into the wood. I liked woods, they made me think of magical things like dwarves and elves and even fairies. The last of these I sort of believed in. Like most hippies I believed that nature spirits were real. These we thought were spirit beings that looked after trees and flowers and cared for the wild things. A healthy tree, we believed, would have good vibes about it and was probably being looked after by several of these good spirits. It was however possible to offend these spirits so that they would attack you. It was with this fear in mind that I walked deeper into the cold, misty wood at dusk. I nervously trod the crisp ground and with every step the sound of cars became more distant and muffled, and the crunching of my feet got louder and louder, until that was the only sound there was.

I unshouldered my rucksack, plopped it on the ground, and then started to build my tent. It wasn't difficult to put up, just a bit of a nuisance when you were tired and cold. I got in and climbed into my sleeping bag. The ground was lumpy and, despite my clothes, the cold was seeping up from the earth below. I realised that I could only just hear the cars on the motorway. This served to remind me how far away I was from help if I needed it. Even though I was in no actual danger and even though I valued the solitude, I still felt very alone and very vulnerable. Part of me was of course afraid of having offended the nature spirits, and that they might wreak some dark revenge on me, perhaps for having trodden oaf-like on some tiny sapling that they had spent several years tenderly nurturing. I did not sleep peacefully or comfortably that night as I imagined the nature spirits dive bombing my mind, and as I wrestled with the cold in the constricting confines of my sleeping bag.

I woke not very refreshed. Moving like an old man I emptied my bladder. It was light, so it must have been after nine o'clock. I groaned inwardly at the thought of having to pack my tent up. This was always such a chore, especially if you hadn't yet had that all important first cup of tea. I didn't have a camping stove, or tea, so that wasn't an option. Kneeling down on the cold ground I pulled up the tent pegs, dismantled the poles and reluctantly lumped around folding the tent together. I rolled it into a tight cylinder with a certain amount of satisfaction at how well I had compacted it, and then shoved it into its bag. I sat for a few minutes as I was still in a waking up daze. Then, smiting myself into action, I strapped my kit up and made for the motorway. The hiss and rumble of traffic got closer and closer. It sounded good and busy now that the New Year was over. I felt excitement at the prospect of catching the ferry to Calais. Going abroad was still a great and novel thrill for me. The only slight caveat was that I couldn't speak French. Still, I knew that many people abroad spoke English, and some had learnt German, in which I was fairly fluent. So with that in mind, and knowing I always had the fall back position of waving my arms around and talking louder, I wasn't too worried.

I clambered back through the fencing, across the scrub verge and onto the hard shoulder. The pent-up energy from the holiday was showing itself in the amount of traffic. I was a bit concerned that it was in fact too busy. Under these conditions people often didn't stop because it wasn't safe to do so with so much traffic bearing down on them from behind. To my surprise I didn't have to wait long. A small car pulled up about a hundred yards past my position. I gathered up my stuff and ran. This time it was a young couple. They were very smiley, and the girl clearly thought that picking up a hitch-hiker was a really fun thing to do. She seemed to be bouncing with the thrill of it, and gave off feelings of welcome that lifted me and set me up with a positive attitude for the day ahead.

"We're going to Dover," said the lad.

"That's great, that's where I'm heading, thanks."

The girl got out and I climbed into the back of the two door vehicle, feeling a bit cramped with my rucksack bundled in there with me and my knees in a side-saddle position due to lack of leg room. We set off. We picked up speed and slid safely into the traffic.

"How far have you come?" asked the girl.

"I've been camping in the woods, you are my first lift of the day."

"In the woods? Wow! Wasn't it a bit cold?" she asked, sounding a hint impressed.

"Yeh, a bit," I replied.

"Harry's just passed his driving test, we're having a day out in Dover," she explained.

Harry stuck his chin out smugly and smiled. It was a big beaming young smile, the sort that only happy well-adjusted kids make.

They were pleasant company but they were of course 'straights', conformist, blind, mindless automatons of materialistic society. I looked down on them and felt entitled to the lift they were giving me. I sensed that I wasn't going to have a very spiritual conversation with them so I asked them what they did for a living. As I had guessed, both of them were still living at home and both were still studying; she was at school and he was gearing up for University. He wanted to study Physics. A little light went on in my brain when he said this. I had always been interested in science, maybe there was an opening here to talk about things Cosmic. I asked him if he believed in lay lines, and when this drew a blank I explained that they were like power lines of positive life energy criss-crossing the country; that they created fertile landscapes along their routes, and churches and ancient religious sites usually marked their sources and intersections.

"That's interesting," he replied sounding a little dubious, a slight nervous quiver in his voice. He obviously didn't know what to say next so I helped him by explaining that witches and druids often used such sites as energy sources for their magic.

"Is that like astrology?" asked the girl.

"Yes, a bit, they do astrology as well," I replied, exercising tolerance.

They dropped me off an hour later in a busy part of Dover near the dock. By now the girl looked a bit worried, and he sounded nervous and tense. They both wished me well, and bade me a good journey. I hoped my conversation had gone some way to loosening them up a bit and encouraging them into a more creative lifestyle, but I didn't hold out much hope. I waved and they waved back as they pulled away.

After another breakfast that sent my Yin-Yang balance into a tailspin, I looked around Dover for a while. I then bought my ferry ticket for France. The ferry was due to leave at about two o'clock so I had time to kill. I spent it in cafés to keep out of the cold, stretching out cups of tea right down to the last sip before buying another one, or moving on to a different café. I could not do this too often because tea cost money, and I didn't have much of that. I usually waited till I detected that tell-tale glare in the proprietor's eye before moving on.

Eventually, inevitably, departure time approached. I made my way to the docks and passed through customs hoping the border guards would ask me to open my bags and question me.

That would have been fun and it would have been a story to tell. I was disappointed however when they completely ignored me and waved me on. I obviously needed to work on my image somewhat.

Once through the boarding tunnel I went straight to the outside viewing decks and leaned over the railings. This was getting serious. I had travelled abroad alone before but never in winter, and that vulnerable feeling was starting to nag me again. After a short wait I saw the mooring ropes being removed and pulled up, and felt the almost subliminal vibration of the boat's engines as they clenched their muscles and churned up a pretty tonnage of water, pushing the boat away from the jetty. Then a short pause and once again vibrations, and the beginnings of a chaffing wake, as ponderously we set off. Imperceptibly we picked up speed as we passed the harbour's entrance and out onto the open sea. The prow was pointing defiantly toward France, as if remembering centuries of inclement history. The waters were grey and seemed as hard as stone and as sharp as glass. I went to the bow of the ferry; it was smashing through the choppy sea as it reflected the overcast sky above. The boat was on a headlong lumbering gallop towards Calais and high adventure.

Chapter 3

Culturally Reserved

On arriving at Calais I wandered around, not really having any purpose or knowing where I was going. I was behaving a bit like a blind man who didn't know where he was, and so kept bumping into things and then changing course in the hope that he would find a meaningful direction. The most disturbing things about homelessness are not having a place that is safe enough to leave your belongings while you wander around, as well as not having somewhere to go back to, to hide your feelings when necessary. It would have helped if there had been somewhere interesting to go, or if the shops and cafés had had a familiarity to them. But even just across the Channel there was enough alienness of culture to make me feel lost and to compound my feelings of being directionless. I didn't know it at the time but this void-like feeling would be vastly magnified later on in my journey.

It was getting late, so I started once again to hunt for somewhere to sleep.

I eventually found some shrubbery in a park. This involved climbing over a fence. I didn't bother putting my tent up, but instead got into my sleeping bag and wrapped myself in the tent. That night was colder and more uncomfortable than my first night in the haunted wood. The temperature was once again below freezing and the ground was rock hard.

The next morning after getting up and slowly, haltingly packing up my gear, I left the park, this time by the gate. I soon discovered how expensive France was when I bought a croissant and a coffee for my breakfast. Croissants and coffee seemed very 'oo la la' and frilly to me, and they weren't very filling either. How could this pathetic pastry, prone to disintegration as you bit into it, pass as a real breakfast?

My plan was to head south towards the Mediterranean as quickly as possible, to get as far away from this cold weather as I could. I knew it would not be warm at this time of year, even down south, but anything was better than this permanent ice box that I now found myself in.

Again I travelled by motorway. Apart from the slight feeling of wrongness that comes from being on the right side of the road and having oncoming traffic on your left, and some unfamiliar road signs, the biggest difference for me was the toll gates that seemed to be a major feature at every slip road.

On my third night I found myself shivering at one of these toll gates. There was no shop and no services at this toll gate, only a police station.

This was a classic hitch-hiker's nightmare. It always seemed that, in an almost sadistic way, drivers did not give lifts in nasty weather.

It reminded me of similar situations back home that would send me into what I called the 'Bazooka Rage'. You've not truly experienced hitch-hiking until you have experienced the 'Bazooka Rage'. I imagine it takes slightly different forms with different people, but basically it is when you are left at a lonely spot, in lousy weather, early in the morning, in sleet, rain, snow or freezing cold. The occasional car that does appear tantalises you with its slow approach; its headlights, optimistic and bright, promise you warmth and friendship. Then just when you think your suffering is over, your trust is suddenly smitten in the most insulting way as the car, without slowing, drives past you and heads off down the slip road to the motorway, whisking itself away to freedom. Depending on your level of patience, after about the first hour you begin to experience the 'Bazooka Rage'. I have never been in the armed forces so my imaginary bazooka seemed to come straight from my soul. It was natural, the only way to feel what I felt, that rage at the drivers who drove by and left me shivering. I could not help but wish I had a bazooka, and in my mind's eye I did. I would shoot a shell into the back of the receding vehicle imagining the driver's look of distress and regret as he saw the projectile in his rear view mirror heading straight towards him. If he was lucky he died instantly, otherwise his vehicle took a few tumbles and he fell out, flaying his broken limbs; his flame-engulfed body would stagger a few paces then kneel and slowly burn to a shrivel.

The police station that I now found myself next to made me feel uneasy. Even though the more serious minded hippies (if that's not an oxymoron) did not think of themselves as criminals, there can be no doubt that there was a spectrum of people in the hippie culture from extreme idealists right through to hardened criminals.

Criminal types often used the hippie scene's open house ethos as a way of finding accommodation while they were on the run. Most of these were petty crooks who were wanted in other areas of the country, and gave false names and addresses if questioned by the police. This was easy to get away with in an age before computers, where the most sophisticated form of data transfer was probably no more than a fax machine.

We often referred to the police as 'pigs'. I think most of us just did this because it was the done thing, and it earned us some cool points, rather than because we had any sort of visceral hatred of the police.

I for one had only had fleeting contact with the police, and in all cases I had been treated appropriately. I never experienced the beatings that I had heard about from the more criminally orientated members of the hippie scene. Police had often searched me for drugs as I stood hitch-hiking. But I had more sense than to carry anything while I travelled, and they were usually friendly and good humoured. Sometimes I even got a lift while they were checking me out on the radio. They did however represent society in general, and for that reason alone I felt some contempt and suspicion towards them.

French police were a different kettle of fish. I knew this already. They were, I had heard, harsher in their methods than British police, and so I was a little bit afraid to be stuck outside one of their police stations at night. As I stood there even lorry drivers seemed to ignore my pleading looks. I felt like a creature in a pond, as they leaned over their steering wheels and peered down at me from the height of their nice warm cabs while queuing to pay their toll money. Eventually as the night grew colder, I crossed a threshold. I realised that my life, or at least my health, was at risk from possible hyperthermia, so I did the unthinkable. I went to the police station to ask for help. To my surprise they let me sleep on the floor in a spare room. The only sign of hostility was when I was woken in the middle of the night by a policeman who came in and stood astride me while I was in my sleeping bag, pointing his finger at me, sneering and saying something in French. All I caught was 'Engleesh hippeee', then he went out and left me alone.

When I got up in the morning to leave I was all but ignored, and allowed to continue on my journey. Most of the lifts I got were not very interesting from a conversational point of view. They often involved a French person practising their English on me. I got the feeling that French people looked down on the English, almost as if the English hadn't yet got past the stage of grunting and snorting around their caves. To me they seemed to constantly have their noses in the air and appeared to express disdain for anything that didn't meet their dizzying aesthetic standards. I dreaded to think what would happen if I told them I was German, something along the lines of a boar hunt maybe.

I finally got to Marseille, and while I was in a café I managed to pick out some people who I would have described as sympathetic to the hippie culture. They were easily identifiable by the rock band logos and flower patches sewn onto their denims. These were people who had adopted some of the values of the Sixties pop culture, but had not gone all the way. They retained jobs and stable accommodation, and didn't grow their hair too long. But they loved the music of the Sixties, raved about the Beatles, lived with their girlfriends and sometimes smoked marijuana.

This was a type of sophistication in their eyes, and the French relish the idea of being regarded as sophisticated.

Sympathetic types also tended to have an adventurous attitude towards hospitality, wanting to interact with strange new exotics like myself. Even ones who were apparently English in origin. I ingratiated myself with them as best I could, and managed to get a roof over my head for the night.

I am not sure what I said or did, but by the next day I seemed to have lost my cool credentials. It might just have been that the bubble had burst. The dream of opening your home doesn't always match up to the reality, especially when you start to feel that your privacy is being torn away from you. Anyway I left that morning and carried on travelling, this time in a westerly direction.

On one occasion, while hitch-hiking in Britain, I had been told about what the driver referred to as a 'cultural reserve' in the mountains of southern France. Apparently a small empty village in the Massif Central had been taken over by a couple who had turned it into a place where people could go to write poetry and read T.S. Eliot, and to indulge in other similarly lofty intellectual pursuits. This appealed to me no end. A secluded village that had been taken over by like-minded people, where everything was free and easy, and you spent all day trying to grasp the depths of eloquent verse and the heights of erudite discourse, and maybe your mind would climb to a more transcendental plane in the process. I didn't know anything about T.S. Eliot, but quite a few people had given me the impression that only the best tuned minds could grasp his writings, and so I assumed he must be a pretty cool and spiritual guy. My definition of spiritual at the time had nothing to do with right or wrong, good or bad, instead it was purely based on talent and ability. If you were a brilliant poet then it didn't matter how immoral you were, or how much hurt you caused other people. In my estimation you were a really spiritual guy because of your talent.

The journey to this village involved some small roads and some frustratingly short lifts, but I made it there in the end. The weather in the south of France at that time of year was cold, but nothing like what I had experienced on the journey thus far. It was with a certain amount of relief that I arrived at this remote and secluded mine of astral energy, set in the rocky terrain of boulder-strewn scarps and woodland.

The village was composed of a few diminutive stone buildings, all of which contained small cramped rooms made more so because of the thickness of the walls. To my disappointment the people who ran this place looked a bit straight. Though they were kind enough and gave me a cup of coffee on my arrival, which I accepted gratefully. I looked around uncomfortably at how well organised and well maintained the place looked. I told them why I had come here, that I wanted to study T.S. Eliot and maybe write some poetry of my own. At this they started to look a bit uncomfortable, as did the two guests who were obviously staying there with them. I noticed that the guests were also a bit too straight for my liking, and old, at least 35 years old, with the beginnings of everything pertaining to age. Waistlines that were starting to tub out a bit, or arms that were starting to dry and become a bit twiggy. All movement and speech was sensible and measured, and their dress, while casual, was not colourful or in any way ideologically radical. None of them had long hair except for one of the women. None wore patches or badges or even jeans.

The older a person was, the less likely it was that they were cool. Mick Jagger was not yet over sixty, neither was this eventuality even imaginable except perhaps in some bizarre parallel universe. The only people with wrinkles who could connect with us hippies were hundreds of years old, and lived as spaced out hermits in remote Himalayan caves.

The Sixties culture was essentially a youth culture. Older people were blamed for pretty much everything that was wrong with the world, and we, the young, were going to wrest the controls from their hands and show them how it was done. The spiritual dimension to this was summed up in the words of another song I loved that told of the dawning of a new age called Aquarius.

I had always found this song stirring, and often I'd stare glassy eyed into the distance hoping for a future in which mankind would not blow itself into oblivion in a cataclysm of blazing, face peeling light, with twisting, roiling mountains of smoke dancing with the agony of the dying, before slowly freezing all life to stone in a nuclear winter that would produce millennia of silence.

This was a very real fear that we all experienced in those days, and it is no exaggeration to say that it hung ominously over absolutely everything we did. Most of us, myself included, believed it was highly unlikely that we would make it past the year 2000 alive.

Only if you were willing to launch your own missiles were you kept 'safe' from the other man's missiles. In the hippie culture we blamed the previous generations for getting us into this dilemma. It was our parents who started World War Two, our grandparents who were responsible for World War One; they and generations before them *ad infinitum* had fought and killed and tortured. They had left us with a world in which nobody could be sure that when they went to bed at night, they would not wake up flaying around in a mass of burning blankets. We were angry, that was for sure. We were terrified, there was no doubt about that. Unlike other wars, this sort could start and you wouldn't even know it, and then it would be over within a matter of minutes, leaving you scorched and blackened, and if you were unlucky, still alive. It's small wonder that some of us searched for escape routes into some sort of nirvana, or even looked for answers in the insanity of drugs.

One of the owners went out of the room. I heard the sound of rummaging; he returned with a book by T.S. Eliot. I accepted it with thanks. At last I had in my hands something that would help me navigate the twisted tracks of my Byzantine mind and clamber up to my inner heaven, that was somehow supposed to be more real than objective reality, which didn't really exist according to the better yogis. I found a quiet spot, even though everywhere indoors was a bit too small and cramped for any real privacy, and I began to read.

I immediately hit a stifling blank, as if my brain was made of heavy grey concrete. To my horror I did not understand a word of what I was reading. Some of the verses had a prettiness to them, and some had a profound sounding lilt implicit in the wording, but I had no idea what they were supposed to be about, and I could make no connection at all with anything in my own experience. I persevered unconsciously, rocking a little as I banged my head against this immovable obstacle. Eventually out of sheer boredom and feeling extremely troubled, I put the book down. Was I so unspiritual as to be unable to make a connection with, so I believed, one of the most profound minds of our time? All of a sudden I felt depressed.

I wandered around a bit. The village was set high up on the side of a wild valley. On the other side of the valley a track wound its way along, echoing the route of the tumbling stream down below it. The village itself was not accessible by tarmac, only by a long dirt road. I felt lifted at the prospect of being able to explore, and at not having to spend too much time with these old, straight people in their over-organised, so-called 'cultural reserve'.

I walked for half an hour along a wooded path on my side of the valley. I liked what I saw, it harked back to more primitive times. There were no electricity pylons, no tarmacked roads, and wild goats hid themselves against the crags and amongst the gorges. After this quick taster I returned to the village, and for want of something better to do I sat in one of the communal areas. Then one of the owners came in to where I was sitting, and with a rictus of a smile on her face, like someone trying to tread on cornflakes without making them crunch, she explained to me that it would cost me several francs to stay the night. Though I remained silent, I was outraged at the blatant capitalism of it all. How could these gross materialists have the audacity to ask me for money for staying in a beautiful place like this? How could they entertain the notion that they owned this wilderness? What made them think that they were allowed to exploit both it and myself in this way? And besides, I was already short of money in a country in which food seemed to cost a fortune.

I was not a political animal and the thought of going to a political rally or a party conference of any stripe did not appeal to me one bit. But my politics, like all hippies, was by default very left wing and paralleled my anti-materialistic spiritual ideas in a very harmonious way. On top of this, I was immature enough to be so idealistic, so as to be completely unrealistic when it came to the implementation of my beliefs, whether political or spiritual.

So, wild eyed and with righteous zeal, I shouldered my rucksack and stomped off gruffly, huffing like an old lady who had just heard a three-year-old swearing.

My plan? To find another abandoned village in these forsaken valleys and make it my hiding place, for quiet meditation, and to soak up the healing vibes of this fresh, cool, uncomplicated place.

As usual I hadn't thought through any of the practicalities, except in the vaguest possible terms. When I found shelter, then I would look for food, was as far as my plan went.

I had no survival training at all, except for a few tips that I remembered from my boy scout days.

But once again I was on the turbulent sea of adventure, and now it was getting real. I was connecting with a wilderness, and I was enjoying the experience, so I moved on stridently up and down the wooded path, along the side of the goat-haunted valley.

I could find no flat spots for my tent, and besides I was starting to hanker after a slightly more permanent roof over my head, at least in the short term.

So I kept going.

There was a pleasant trickling sound coming from the stream below. It was drawing me to climb down and explore its splashing surprises and smooth, cold pools. I didn't give in. I had to find a good shelter before I could afford that kind of distraction. I had been walking for less than 40 minutes and to my total surprise I saw, down in the valley, nestled against the stream, a primitive looking village. Its handful of buildings were in a bad state of repair, and it looked as if it had been tossed randomly onto the irregular terrain next to the stream.

It had no cables, no wires, no tarmac, no paving or any other signs of infrastructure. It was clear to me that this place would have no electricity, no phones, no gas, no mains water and no sewage disposal. It looked as if these houses had remained basically unchanged for hundreds of years. It seemed almost miraculous that people had still been living in such a historically dislocated place less than a decade ago.

How had the primitives who had lived there coped when they finally gave in to the pull of the outside world? Had they had nervous breakdowns as they looked around gob-smacked at a totally alien high speed culture, one that they didn't even begin to understand? Maybe their uncluttered minds and naïve points of view had gleaned some good humoured affection for them from the jaded city dwellers. If they weren't too inbred or nervously fragile, then maybe the sheer sanity and clarity imbibed during a childhood spent living in this petrified past had got them through. It might even have helped them to succeed in a sick, tangled world as they plodded the road of some robust and stalwart wisdom learnt from these unforgiving boulders.

I sat on the path and looked down on the buildings for a while. It was ideal.

Though when I looked more closely, I was disappointed to see possible signs of habitation.

There were cats hanging around near one of the houses.

And was that something laid out to dry on a rock? The day was cold but sunny.

Was that a bucket parked by a door?

Sure enough, moments later, someone did come out of one of the houses. It was a girl in her early twenties.

My heart sank, my dream of solitude was demolished, especially when she was followed out by a young bearded blond haired man in his late twenties.

But as I watched I realised that they didn't look particularly straight. His hair was tied back in a ponytail. Both of them wore dowdy, rough clothes echoing the clothing that the former inhabitants of this place would have worn while going about their daily tasks.

I was a bit miffed that they had got there first, but decided it might be fun to introduce myself anyway. So I scrambled down the side of the valley till I was level with the stream.

It wasn't difficult to find stepping stones to hop across the stream. By now they had noticed me and were standing staring at me as I approached them.

"Hello," I called as I walked towards them, hoping they had learnt English at school. In fact, given the location, wondering if they had been to school at all.

"Ello," came the promising but not yet conclusive reply.

"Do you live here?" I asked. An idiotic question, but I couldn't think of anything else to say.

"This is where we live, yes. You are walking?"

To my relief I realised he must at least have a basic grasp of English.

"No, I am looking for somewhere to stay," I replied. "Are any of these buildings empty?"

"Most are derelict," he informed me.

After a few moments of awkward silence, he and his girlfriend moved back towards their house and went inside. They left the door open which I took to be a hint. I paused a moment in the doorway before going in. Both were sitting on the floor; only the girl looked up as I walked in. She did not smile but neither was her expression hostile.

The ground storey of their house consisted of one room with a packed dirt floor. The walls were daubed with some kind of simple white plaster that made them look relatively flat. This was in surprisingly good condition. The most sophisticated thing in the room was a wooden ladder leading up to the loft that constituted the top floor. The second most sophisticated thing was the plain open hearth area for a fire, which had been built into one of the walls. There was not a hint of piping or wiring in sight; no switches, taps, radiators, aerials, carpets, chairs, tables or pictures. Just a flapping plank door that let the wind and light in under its rotted base.

They both sat facing the hearth. I sat down next to them. The hearth had the smouldering remains of a wood fire, and a bit of smoke blew my way making me cough, while at the same time invoking that difficult to define comfort that wood smoke tends to bring to the surface in most people.

"Are you from here?" I asked.

"Paris," came the one word answer.

Great! I thought. *Hippies at last.*

I had been a bit worried that I had landed among some peasant types, towards whom it would have been compulsory that I as a hippie should feel admiration and not a little spiritual awe. In truth I knew that I would have had difficulty figuring out what to talk about, and trouble respecting their simple, gawping, toothless smiles.

There was an aloofness about the man, but not so much the girl. She was not enamoured with me, I could tell, but she seemed to be willing to accommodate me, while at the same time looking nervously to him for her cues. I told them where I was from and in my usual self-destructive way I also admitted to my German heritage.

During the war some people thought of Hitler as the anti-Christ. Hippies had similar feelings, they tended to see him as the ultimate anti-hippie. Clearly I knew how to make things difficult for myself. What was already a cold situation suddenly became even colder. The young man still spoke to me, but it was in a stilted, stunted, attenuated manner. He seemed to grit his teeth and lean back a bit as he spoke.

As usual I took this to heart. accepting the guilt of my people and somehow implying it onto myself, as well as hating my mother for anything she might have caused me to imbibe by her proximity during my childhood years.

Despite having caused a bit of extra tension, I eventually learnt that his name was Lucas and that she was called Claire.

Looking around I noticed that there was no food in the room except for a few burnt chestnuts next to the fire. I suddenly realised that I was feeling hungry. In fact very hungry, not having eaten since breakfast time. I had been so busy exploring my new environment and ingratiating myself with these people that the need for food had crept up on me slowly without my being aware of it. As I've already mentioned I don't have the sort of metabolism that stores fat. So being an energetic young person, when I did get hungry I was often ravenous, my body crying out to be refuelled as soon as possible, since it had no reserves to fall back on. Knowing it was uncool to be too concerned about eating, and very conscious of my low esteem in their eyes, I nevertheless did ask if they had anything to eat.

Lucas nodded towards a pan of boiling water on the fire. There was a herbal smell coming from it. "We drink marjoram tea."

After a long five minutes watching the pan, Claire climbed the ladder and brought down three tin mugs. She poured the tea, first giving a mug to him, then placing one in front of herself, and after that handing one to me. I had never had marjoram tea before. Herbal tea was still a bit of a novelty in those days, even amongst hippies. It smelt pleasant but it was obviously not going to quell my hunger.

I knew better than to ask if there was any sugar.

"Are the chestnuts from the woods?" I asked.

"Claire collects them, they are left over from autumn," he told me.

"Is there anything else to eat out there?"

"No," came the short reply.

"Sometimes we find mushrooms. In autumn there are berries."

To the Western mind starvation is never an option, but these people seemed not just to have accepted it, but to have embraced it.

Racked with guilt I started to calculate distances and times to the nearest shops. My dreams of living in seclusion close to nature were starting to sink into the quicksand of reality. I had hoped to train my appetites gradually, rather than have hunger and need thrust upon me in such an uncontrolled way.

This was not the first time I had tried to connect with the wilderness. About nine months earlier I had gone to the Lake District. It was March, and there were still some patches of snow on the hills. My aim was similar to what I was trying to do here in France.

I had intended to find a place in the hills, far away from other people, to meditate. At the time I was a strict vegetarian and I was also involved in macrobiotics. Macrobiotics is supposed to be about eating a balanced diet that is neither too Yin (feminine) nor Yang (masculine).

According to the practitioners of this Buddhist discipline, 'You are what you eat'. If you are off balance in either direction this makes you less spiritual, and leads to behavioural problems and eventually bodily sickness.

According to the ancients, brown rice was the perfect food for achieving this balance, and not just brown rice, but raw brown rice, each mouthful being chewed at least fifty times. You could cleanse your body and balance your psyche by spending several weeks, or even a lifetime, eating nothing but brown rice. In theory it didn't matter what food you ate, so long as the Yin-Yang balance was maintained, but brown rice was billed as being the fast lane to mental stability, spirituality and peace of mind.

I had gone into the Cumbrian hills carrying my two bags of raw brown rice, looking forward to a few weeks of serenity, while my mind fed on the beauty and tranquillity of my surroundings. I had identified a disused mine or quarry of some sort, on my Ordnance Survey map. It appeared to have some derelict buildings marked on it. I knew that habitable caves would be difficult to find, so derelict buildings would have to do. I also carried a tent, so I could strike out if I wanted to.

When I got there I found some old mine buildings of corrugated iron construction in the bottom of the valley. These looked as if they might contain deep, deadly shafts hidden by rotting planks that were originally supposed to make them safe. Apart from that, they also looked draughty, as the bent and detached corrugated sheets flapped in the cold wind. I didn't bother exploring them even though deep holes hold the same fascination for me that they do for most people.

Higher up I could see what looked like concrete bunkers. They were simple rectangular constructions and they ran the length of a ledge that had been cut halfway up the side of the valley. I was not far from the head of the valley, and getting to these bunkers involved negotiating the edge of a tall, wide crag that had a small stream flowing over its brim. After doing this I had to climb up a steep scree slope.

As I scrambled up the last bit of scree onto the ledge, I sat down to get my breath back and take in the view. Then because it was getting colder and starting to darken, I checked out the bunkers. Neither had doors nor windows, just empty sockets. Both smelt a bit of urine and contained pieces of random litter and the remnants of small fires. The old fires were nothing but black splodges of damp ash on the floor; one had a beer bottle next to it. I found a corner that was both out of the draught and didn't smell of urine, and wrapped myself up in my sleeping bag and my tent, ready for a hard, cold, grey night ahead.

Despite being wrapped up well, the draught eventually found me. It tickled the fine hairs on the back of my neck, somehow getting its long flexible finger down to my skin. No amount of padding, wrapping or pillowing could stop it. In the end I just accepted its cold blade touching my back as it worked its way down my spine.

I didn't sleep well. When I finally got up I looked down at the floor and concluded that concrete did not make for a very good mattress.

I should have been able to sleep anywhere.

Didn't the yogis sit naked on top of freezing rocks in the Himalayas and find Nirvanic joy in the process?

Much as I hated to admit it I was still a long way from that.

And what about the Chinese and the Japanese? I had heard that they actually preferred to sleep on hard floors.

What was wrong with me?

I threw my arms in the air in dismay.

I would have to give this some serious thought.

I had risen early because of the cold. Dawn was still a vague smudge atop the mountains, so I climbed back into my sleeping bag, which for just a moment felt warm, but soon became cold again. I would have to wait another hour or two for the temperature to improve so that I could begin to explore.

When daylight did eventually come, I began to chew my brown rice while studying the valley below. I soon realised that breakfast was going to take a very long time at fifty chews per mouthful, but I persisted and prevailed.

I was very bored. Even though I had sought it diligently, I could not find anything particularly wholesome or holy in the flavour of the rice. If it had tasted bad that might have helped, but it was just bland, and chewing it was incredibly tedious.

A couple of days dragged by. I ate snow for my thirst and longed for a little salt to cheer up my diet.

The thought of a cup of tea was unbearable, my gagging need for it was suggestive of addiction.

I had spent days eating brown rice before, but never raw, and never combined with sleeping rough, with loneliness, and with boredom. I tried making up mystical sounding names for the various features in the valley, but the names were so mystical that I forgot them almost immediately. Calling a rock Llografidle, or a stream Splagachin, is a bit futile if you forget what you called it five minutes later.

On impulse I packed up my tent and sleeping bag and went in search of better vibes somewhere else. I walked over the brow at the end of the valley and started down the other side, into the top part of another wild, harsh, rocky valley. After continuing for a while I halted and set up my tent on a low-lying flat spot.

I knew there was a farmhouse on the open lands about three miles further along, where the mountains melted into pasture, but at this point I didn't give it much thought.

When night came it started to pour down with rain that repeatedly slapped my tent, as the wind hurled great lashes of water in my direction. The tent began to sag and leak and topple under the weight of rain plummeting from the sky. I was soon lying in a saturated sleeping bag, with the slick wet canvas across my face, wondering if I should be a good yogi and detach myself from my bodily desires, or if I should perhaps go and ask somebody for help. Call it common sense, call it cowardice, I did eventually give in. In the early hours of the morning I struggled through the storm down to the farmhouse beyond the valley's end. In my drenched bedraggled state with my long hair stringy and plastered to my scalp and face, running its own tiny streams down my plastic anorak, I knocked on the farmhouse door. Happily it was the farmer not his wife who answered. I told him my dilemma and asked him if he could give me shelter till the weather passed. He put me in one of his barns and told me to wait there for him. It was a while before he returned. I imagine he had been ringing the police to check that I wasn't an escaped convict, or someone with a dangerous mental illness, running loose in the hills. When he did return he had with him a full English breakfast. I looked at it, the two fried eggs stared up at me hypnotically. This was the sort of situation in which Buddha would have had a meltdown, his inexplicably tubby body dripping grease everywhere.

If I had thought about it I would have realised that his belly could be taken as tacit permission to do whatever you like – eat, don't eat, it's all the same, and a clear nod to amorality for anyone who could see it. How many corrupt and overweight monks had found comfort in, and been furnished with excuses, by his cheerful and chubby demeanour?

Wrapped in a blanket I ate. I was almost comatose with bliss when I had my first sip from that lovely mug of hot sweet tea.

He still kept me in the barn though, and I never did meet his wife.

Lucas and Claire let me have a couple of chestnuts. Despite my hunger they tasted bland. I discovered that while he could speak English in an uncomfortable stilted sort of way, she had no English at all. We nevertheless managed to converse about our respective views and beliefs. His beliefs were actually very compatible with my own, in fact his beliefs were to a large extent an extreme form of my own beliefs, if that were possible. Or maybe it would be more accurate to say that he had gone further down the road when it came to implementing those beliefs.

It turned out that they had a philosophy of living from day to day, and not worrying where their next meal came from. Lucas justified this by quoting the Bible when Jesus said: "Therefore I tell you, do not worry about your life, what you will eat or drink or about your body, what you will wear." This he coupled with the idea that if you don't worry about it, it will come to you, but if you do worry about it, you will go hungry. So rather than having faith in God to supply these things, he believed that you needed to have faith in faith to supply these things. This suited me fine, since I did not want to believe in a God who was a person, and loving, and so held me responsible for my life of unloving actions and attitudes. I was hiding from this light by not believing these things, but I soon found that having faith in faith is a bit like trying to climb a slippery pole, especially if you are the sort of person who cannot entirely throw caution to the wind, or have the sort of nervous mind that always checks the shadows.

There was also a strong political bent to Lucas's thinking, and he was very left wing.

It was as if, through these people, I was having the implications of my own extremism thrown back in my face. I in my self-righteousness had turned my nose up at the people living in the 'cultural reserve', and now I found myself in a situation in which these people were likely to reject me because I could not keep up with them in their radical lifestyle. The extent to which they were willing to follow this path was clear, in that she was pregnant. They seemed to have rejected anything to do with modern society and comfortable living in favour of a simplicity that included starvation.

To Lucas, if you had enough food stored up for the next day, you were a capitalist and something that strongly resembled a disgusting, fat, blood-bloated leech, thrashing its blind head about seeking flesh to latch onto. To justify this point he again quoted the Bible and Jesus: "Therefore do not worry about tomorrow, for tomorrow will worry about itself. Each day has enough trouble of its own."

Lucas appeared to have a bit of a Messiah-complex, and it was obvious by the way that she looked at him that Claire had bought into this. A mild expression of fear and adoration occasionally betrayed her feelings when she glanced towards him. This attraction was clearly psychological since he was not impressively built. There was however a certain intelligence implied in his features.

On one occasion we did take some initiative to find food, even though Lucas probably didn't see it in those terms. We walked down to the nearest town a few miles away. There was a small supermarket there. We rummaged through the waste at the back of the supermarket and found semi-rotten fruit and similar items to eat. At the time this seemed like a feast.

At each conversation I had with Lucas he fed my feelings of guilt and inadequacy. He would have made a great cult leader, and who knows, maybe that's what he became. Despite the fact that he quoted the Bible, his thinking tended to move more along political than spiritual lines. He appeared to share the contempt for religion that a lot of French people have, while elevating politics and art in a way that turns them into a kind of surrogate religion. He was aloof and scorned anyone who didn't meet his exacting standards. His belief that a person's needs will provide themselves was of course a spiritual belief, but it was cold and impersonal, more along the lines of an evolutionary law of nature than evidence of a benevolent presence in the universe. His politics were so harsh that they had the smell of the gulag, and to me his soul was full of cold, grey concrete blocks. Maybe because this resonated so strongly with the emptiness in my own soul; his influence over me grew rather than diminished, as I sensed both hardness and stimulating anger inside of him.

After several days of this indoctrination I became racked with guilt and was determined to make myself more spiritual. So I took my rucksack and walked some of the way back along the woodland track. I left my rucksack complete with sleeping bag, money and tent where it could be found. I hoped it would be found by Lucas and Claire. Then I walked off in nothing but the clothes I was wearing, leaving my coat behind with the rucksack, because owning a coat was far too materialistic.

Chapter 4

There is Nothing to Fear but Fear

It was a bit like learning to ride a bicycle with squealing cats leaping across your field of vision at random intervals. Or being told that the dog will not attack you provided you are not afraid of it. I spent the first night huddled shivering against a stone wall, trying not to worry about the fact that the universe was not flowing in my direction. I was out in the open somewhere, and I was travelling towards the Spanish border. The warmth of Africa seemed very appealing to me at this point in time. It was indisputably cold, but at least it wasn't British cold. I wasn't going to die of exposure, just of despair. Clearly my thin pullover was not up to the job, even in the south of France.

Exhausted and not having slept a wink I started to hitch-hike as soon as there was a bit of light and the chance of a passing car. During my next lift it was as if my jaw was being controlled by powerful hydraulic pistons. I just could not keep the conversation from eventually arriving at the subject of my current poverty, as if that wasn't already blatantly obvious. The more I tried not to worry about my situation the more I worried about it, with the additional worry that I was worrying about worrying about it. I did not enjoy that lift, and I wasn't particularly scintillating company for the driver either. Having broken a cardinal rule and mentioned my lack of resources, I felt more like a bedraggled beggar than like some elevated yogi who is blinded to the world by his own lofty wisdom, and who is no longer the victim of cause and effect because of his immaculate self control.

Miraculously I had had the sense not to leave my passport behind with my other belongings, so I did not anticipate any problems at the border. But that was not to be. Seeing a tired looking hippie slouching up to the border, without even a plastic carrier bag or a coat to his name, probably raised a few questions and not a few suspicions. I answered honestly when asked if I had any money, and as if to prove to me that honesty is not always a ticket to leniency – and should not be indulged in unless you are willing to accept the consequence – I was refused entry to Spain.

My deranged plans had just been rearranged. The Sahara desert would have to wait a little longer for my bones. I elected to try the long way round. The Middle East was out, because I knew there were always wars going on there, and I didn't want to walk straight into one. I figured that if I could get as close as possible to Africa by land, then maybe I could hitch a lift across the Mediterranean on a fishing boat or something. The nearest land to Africa that I knew about was Sicily, so I did an about turn and left Spain to the Spanish – I don't think they minded too much.

During the lifts that followed I once again tried not to drop hints that I was penniless, even though my appearance and lack of a rucksack were actually very big hints. But that irresistible compulsion to steer the conversation onto the subject made me wonder if my brain was stuck on some sort of inescapable neural railway track. I felt as if I was a totally deterministic entity, as if someone was using crow bars and levers to make me say certain things. I seemed to be some kind of human shaped automaton. The very anxiety that I might reveal my need seemed to forcibly propel me into revealing that very need. As usual I was tormented by guilt, and the dark feelings of failure and inadequacy that ran in long strata right down to the core of my being.

However as I travelled somehow I got by.

This was through a combination of other people's compassion, my own frequent hints, some occasional begging, and now and again going a bit hungry. At one point I picked some unripe oranges on a city avenue, and was gently rebuked by a non-English speaking citizen. I think I must have broken a rule of some sort, the oranges probably belonged to the council. Happily I was not arrested for this, and I continued on my way.

As I travelled, I found that I could sit at the counter in Italian motorway service stations and drink the free water, while raiding the bowl of nuts put out for the customers. Nobody challenged me when I did this, even though it was always obvious to the bar staff what I was up to.

By the time I got to Rome I had all but given up on the universe smiling at me and handing me a sandwich. I was once again a full time beggar. I found my way to a plaza in the depths of the city and made myself comfortable on the steps of a plinth supporting a metal statue of a guy with little wings on his ankles, looking as if he was stepping out of the bath and had just slipped on a bar of soap. I was drawn to this spot because there were a handful of sullen looking hippie dropouts already sitting there. How could I tell that they were hippie dropouts? Certain ways of dressing and attitudes towards personal grooming were more than just fashion statements in those days. Looking rough and unshaven with torn jeans and long hair had not been dictated to us by some super giant fashion house wishing to inflate its profits yet further by freeing us of the burden of our hard earned cash. No. We were the real job, it was on us that in later years the super giant fashion houses wishing to inflate their profits yet further based certain fashion archetypes. If it hadn't been for us they would still be promoting suits and ties, and casual wear would never have got past the polo-neck jumper. We were the generation who invented cool. Really. No kidding.

I scrounged money from passers-by, and I fed myself mainly on pizzas. Back then pizza was not the commonplace international food that it is today. Pizzas were largely seen as an Italian food, and eating a pizza was still an exotic experience to someone like me, who had been born in the land of fish and chips.

While in Rome I met a girl. She was Italian, and clearly very straight, but I was willing to overlook that troubling detail because she was pretty. I got talking to her while browsing some colonnades. Even though her English was close to nonexistent she seemed to like the idea of formally strolling around Rome with me. I could tell that she saw some sort of latent potential in me. She reminded me a lot of my first girlfriend whose Catholicism had got in the way of me satisfying my baser urges with her. I could tell that, just like my previous girlfriend, she was eyeing me up like some master sculpture, wondering what she could bring out of this crude looking lump of rock.

However around about that time my behaviour took a bizarre turn for the worse. I had found a length of sackcloth amongst some rubbish, and decided this would be a good device for making a righteous statement. I needed to tell the world that I was a poverty stricken yogi who didn't need society and all its superficiality. I strode around Rome wrapped in my sackcloth displaying my super spiritual credentials for all to see. As I have already said I am fundamentally a shy person, so a part of me really didn't enjoy the interest I was accruing, even though some of the quick glances I was getting appeared to contain a level of approval. At that stage in my life I had very little idea of how such behaviour might appear to the Catholic mindset. I did not realise that some of those who saw me might have thought that I was a monk or a priest who had taken a vow of poverty, and was doing penance by displaying his humility before the world, and maybe in the process would receive a pat on the head from the Pope.

My ragged garb did manage to get me at least one meal. I was sitting on a doorstep in a street lined with shops that had tall terraced accommodations above them. All of a sudden something landed with a 'phwack' and a 'tinkle' in front of me. It was a paper bag. A few coins had come bouncing out of it as a result of its high velocity impact with ground. Cautiously, I leaned forward and twisted my head as I looked out and upwards from my cover. A young girl in her early teens was smiling down at me. She was surrounded by even younger children, all of whom were laughing and waving. I picked up the bag, gathered the coins, and waved my thanks in return. The bag contained various cakes, some rolls, cheese, apples, an orange and enough money to buy me two more meals.

I couldn't help asking myself *Was I starting to harmonise with the cosmos? Was I evolving into a higher being?* I lived in hope.

My relationship with my new girlfriend didn't last long. Two or three days, and then her common sense or maybe her mother got the better of her. I was sitting at the plinth wearing my sackcloth, a hippie amongst hippies, feeling quite superior, when she marched up to me. She appeared to have a male companion in tow, though he hung back. Primarily with body language and gesticulation she made it clear to me that it was over, before marching off again.

I had not invested a lot of emotion in this short relationship, so this was not too much of a blow to me. Besides, she didn't have enough in common with me for it to go anywhere, at least not in the direction I wanted it to go.

I was really looking for a chick to travel with me – that's right, a 'chick'. The term sounds outrageous in this day and age, but that is what we hippies used to the call the young flower-strewn women who drifted and swirled around dreamily in our alternative cosmos. What is more, they didn't seem to mind being compared to small, cute, fluffy endearing things. Today such a term would solicit a tomahawk in the brain from some harpy in a business suit. However I can't help thinking that the term 'chick' is much better than the more recent term 'bitch'. Maybe today's women would rather be seen as snarling attack dogs than as objects of affection, to be protected by some stubble festooned, muscular, sweaty male. I don't think the term 'bitch' lasted very long anyway. Which is reassuring.

It was growing late, so after scrounging some money and eating a few slices of pizza, I went back to a large cardboard box that I had found down a small side street. This was big enough to contain me and was full of packing material, so I curled up in it and, like a hamster, I went to sleep. The weather was starting to get a bit more friendly, but shelter was definitely still necessary for a comfortable night's rest.

Discarding my sackcloth, I left Rome and carried on down towards Sicily hoping to find a fishing boat to give me a lift to Tunisia. Once in Sicily I spent one night sleeping under an upturned rowing boat before arriving the next evening at Palermo.

I immediately started looking in shop doorways and alleys hoping to find a place that was out of sight so that I could sleep undisturbed, and that was also sheltered from any sea breeze that had found its way into the city. There were still a few people around, and somebody noticed me popping in and out of secluded locations searching for my ideal spot.

I heard a voice behind me. "English, yes? Beatles, yes?" It was a young Italian man probably a few years older than me. "Beatles," he said again. I nodded vigorously. "Yes, Beatles," sensing that this was an opportunity I didn't want to miss. He was dressed in slacks and wore a slimline pullover. My first impression was of a young trendy, similar to the ones I'd met in

Marseille. He was obviously a little sycophantic towards anything or anyone connected with the Beatles. In his eyes since I was a hippie and English, I shone with psychedelic glory. He led the way to his small Italian car, like a waiter showing me to my table. He wore an ingratiating smile and with the occasional nod of his torso he affirmed his desire to serve. He was clearly thrilled with his catch and I was proudly bundled into his car with his two friends. None of them could speak any English that was worth mentioning, but they seemed to like the idea of having me in the car with them.

To me this situation was a first class meal ticket if ever I saw one.

He drove me straight to his flat which was still in the city and not far from the docks. His friends had decided to go home, so the two of us ascended the stairs to the second floor. He kept turning around as if to check that I was still there. His girlfriend had heard us coming and opened the door. They conversed in Italian as she eyed me over. She seemed satisfied, and so they both encouraged me to come in. She had no English at all, but with pointing and nodding and the occasional over emphasised Italian word, she showed me where the coffee was stored and where the milk was kept. I noticed that there was plenty of long life milk in the cupboards as she walked me around the flat like an estate agent looking for a good sale.

Like all good Beatles fans Andrea smoked marijuana, and his stash was quite impressive. He had several large chunks. This I knew was one of the surest ways to get myself back into cigarette smoking. It was possible to smoke marijuana neat, in a pipe or a chillum, but more often than not it was smoked in a joint where it was mixed with tobacco, and to me tobacco was of course a highly addictive substance.

I have heard it suggested in recent years that marijuana itself can be addictive, but to us in the seventies people who made those sort of assertions were the butt of all our jokes.

Andrea rolled a joint and we got stoned. I recognised that hollow euphoric sensation that always comes with marijuana, and is so aptly described by the term 'spaced out'. In my emotions I felt like a balloon being inflated. I am a nervous individual especially in social situations, and along with other things, such anxieties always become magnified under the influence of marijuana. As well as fears being blown up and stretched, so are more pleasant experiences such as music, flavour, colour and sex. It was always hard to say if these experiences were enhancements or just exaggerations, running along some single and simplistic dimension of the mind. The scoffing laughter that smoking marijuana usually produces suggests intelligent comedy and caricature, and one wonders if those who say that it makes a person more creative were thinking of this as their verification. Marijuana did seem to make life into one big cartoon, where prominent features in a person or a situation became exaggerated.

But something was always lost. That empty, airy centre always spoke volumes to any soul who was truly looking for more rather than less; for substance rather than fantasy. There was an insincerity to the hippie scene that I had sensed all along, but that I wasn't willing to admit to just yet. Drugs, while compulsory badges of membership, had always struck me as very artificial. To my simplistic spirituality that which was natural was good, and that which was artificial was bad. So drugs didn't fit into my value system too well, not if I really though it through honestly. Drugs always seemed to be more about having a laugh and discarding truth to the wind, rather than seeking deep and substantial enlightenment. The need for absolute truth was making its demands on me, even before I was willing to acknowledge its intrusive existence. The ghostly vacuousness of smoking marijuana was just one of the things that was making me long for the very objective reality that I was working so hard to deny.

So we drank coffee and we got stoned and then the strangest thing happened, Andrea and his girlfriend got up and with his very limited English, Andrea explained to me that they were going away for a few days, and that I could stay in their flat if I wanted to. And then they were gone! I was left feeling dazed and a bit muddled. This really was open house non-materialistic living. They might have been a bit straight looking but they were certainly walking the walk, not just talking the talk. The first thing I did was check the cupboards for food. I was disappointed. There was plenty of long life milk and coffee and even dried pasta, but nothing that amounted to a proper meal. I would have to scrounge food by begging on the street. I also needed cigarettes for making joints. They had left me with all their marijuana, enough to keep me stoned for a couple of weeks. He must have had a good supplier, and it must have been cheap, otherwise I doubt he would have been so cavalier in his generosity. In Britain, that much marijuana would have been well worth breaking up into a batch of small 'quid deals' to sell on to other people. A quid deal, as the name implies, was sold for £1, and was about the size of a small dice. Usually it was wrapped in silver paper salvaged from a cigarette packet. You could make about three or four joints out of one quid deal.

Making a good joint was a very real skill and I was a pretty reasonable joint engineer. When you are new to making joints what you create tends to fall apart, annoying everybody by dropping chunks of white hot marijuana onto their laps and making them flap about like demented banshees until the drug rearrests their brains and calms them down again. My joints were tight, but not so tight that they didn't draw. Like anything that burns, a joint needs oxygen to work properly. Joints were normally made with several cigarette papers. Though one paper joints were not completely unheard of, it was more usual to make a joint out of three, five or even seven cigarette papers. The 'roach', or the mouth piece of the joint, was just a rolled up bit of cardboard shoved in at the back end of the joint to stop it collapsing as the paper got wet with use, and to act as a small collection chamber for the smoke as you drew on it. If the marijuana was in a resin form – that is, concentrated – then you heated it on a spoon or knife over a flame to soften it and make it more crumbly. That way it became easy to mix evenly with the tobacco. The mixture was spread along the length of the construction of cigarette papers and rolled carefully into shape. Then the papers had to be licked and stuck. Finally the end was twisted closed in a way that made the item unmistakable as anything other than a joint. The twist usually flared a bit when you first lit up.

I practised my joint making skills, and found pleasure in the smooth, unwrinkled cylinders that would have been regarded as aerodynamic in any other context.

They were inverted rockets for the mind. At least that was the opinion of most of those who claimed to believe there was an intellectual or a spiritual dimension to getting stoned.

I explored near to the flat. There were the usual coffee shops and pizza bars, and plazas with statues of men and women in various stages of nudity that forced you to question your own fitness; even the incomplete ones left you with issues. Many of the streets were narrow, overshadowed by balconies and all the hicklety-picklety that always seems to be associated with them – cables, shutters, washing lines, flag poles, canopies, flower baskets.

It was as if history herself was trying to slow this place down by cramping its style and holding Palermo's people to its ample Italian bosom.

A lot of what I was seeing was no longer exotic or novel to me, I was starting to get bored. Any true connoisseur of Italian culture would have had nothing but contempt for me. Despite the fact that there were still volumes of history and forests of aesthetic nuance for me to delve into, I was already starting to suffer from that irritating, prodding need to move on.

Going to the nearby docks I surveyed the ships, and that is exactly what they were – ships. Most of them loomed over me so that my head was at ninety degrees while I was trying to assess them.

I had had in mind a small fishing vessel with a couple of friendly sun roasted Italians bobbing on the Mediterranean, myself helping them pull in the nets, and they in return dropping me off on a quiet North African beach.

I asked a few passing men about jobs on the ships. One of the ships was going to Hong Kong. I considered the prospect of going that far, but the idea of being trapped in the ship's galley washing dishes for days on end, trying not to puke into the suds while I was learning my sea legs, didn't really appeal to me. It was also obvious that these leviathans were not going to pull up on a beach and let me off should the whim overtake me to disembark.

I imagine Palermo had plenty of boats both large and small, but for some reason I didn't bother to look any further. I don't know why, maybe something had broken loose in my brain with all that marijuana smoking; maybe that small part of me that made plans and devised strategies had decided to sit down, fold its hands and study the ceiling.

After Andrea and his girlfriend came back I stayed a few more days, smoked some more marijuana with them, and then left. Andrea was kind enough to give me a sleeping bag. The sleeping bag acted as a sort of teddy bear to cling to in my emotional vacuum, so that my arms didn't flay about wildly looking for something to grab hold of to stop me falling. A sleeping bag, a rucksack, a few small possessions to focus my attention and to call my own. The very act of having something to defend as one's own seems to provide a feeble sense of having a home. It was a piece of wood to cling to in the vast ocean that I was drifting in. A raft would have been better than a piece of wood, and an island better than a raft, but it was something, and it gave me a tiny bit of emotional orientation.

I had no plan. I simply headed north with a view to moving further east. My actions were becoming more obsessive now. I was leaning forward with blind determination to go I knew not where, and to do I knew not what. I was staggering on and reaching out for ghosts in a snow storm. Using the same combination of begging and scrounging as before, I eventually got to the Italy-Yugoslavia border.

Chapter 5

The Portentous Road

Somehow I managed to make the choice to head for Greece. Greece painted a pleasant, clean picture in my mind, of white marble columns and bleached togas, of blue skies and crested waves, of rhythmic, stamping and pally dancing to the strident twanging of a Mediterranean banjo, on a breezy vine-shaded patio by the sea. Where sturdy old men join in with the familial revelry to prove their ongoing virility, as children are knocked over by laughter. Where women feign lofty scoffing, while sullen young men look endearingly insecure. Where girls in plain dresses, not too showy, not too not, huddle in the semi-shadow of a whispering corner, absorbed in barbed giggling, and wafting as if to rid themselves of a bad odour. They are enjoying their moment of power before marriage captures them, and their husbands have final and despotic dominion.

It was misty at the Yugoslav border and there was a long queue of lorries. The drivers were sitting on their thrones in their well-lit cabs. Just as at the toll gate in France, they looked down at me from on high as I walked around their vehicles begging for a lift. As I have said, in Britain a lorry meant at least a one in three chance of a lift. Here the rules seemed to be different. Most of these were bigger that the average British lorry and all had bunk beds behind the seating in the cab. It could have been that many of these lorries were going long haul and didn't want to be left with the choice of dropping me somewhere inhospitable or having me tag along for several days. Despite persistent effort, during which, in my desperation, I probably asked the same drivers several times over, I was consistently turned down. I had to spend the night in the cab of a large tractor parked at the border that someone had neglected to lock. It wasn't too cold anymore;

the mist was a sign of the weather starting to warm up a bit, but I was uncomfortable sleeping upright on the seat. The next day it was still misty and I started to worry that the claustrophobic, imprisoning greyness might be a never-ending feature in this place. I knew that boredom and depression would set in very soon if I didn't get away to somewhere that was more visually stimulating and entertaining. I plodded around like a ghost in Hades. Good cheer seemed to have been banished from this place, and laughter was probably illegal. The lights of the drivers' cabs were harsh blobs floating in the fog, and the drivers could have been demons tending the dead with torment from their podiums whenever some casual whim aroused them.

Then all of a sudden I was successful. A lorry driver beckoned me to climb up into his cab. He was a friendly Frenchman. My experience of French people so far had not been good, however this man clearly radiated geniality. He could not speak English but, feeling a bit like a chimpanzee, I once again found that it was possible to speak volumes just using sign language. The queue was long, but in small lurches we eventually got to the border buildings. Our papers and passports were checked, and in the harsh light of the checkpoint a mist wrapped figure waved us on. The lorry lurched forwards as the driver cycled through his gears, and we were off. Because of the mist progress was slow at first, but the view soon began to clear, giving tantalising glimpses of the occasional rural dwelling. These were the sort of buildings you might expect to find in a communist country, a bit run down and hinting at a kind of modern peasantry. It got lighter and lighter and my own mood rose and rose, gliding upwards into the brightness. After being stuck somewhere for a long time, that rumbling and bumping of a good lift under your bum is always a great joy. And rumbling and bumping is exactly what it was. The roads in Yugoslavia were in an appalling state of repair; there were potholes everywhere, and all too frequently we came across car wrecks on the side of the road, some of them completely burnt out.

The national sport seemed to be seeing how many animals you could run over. There were dead dogs, dead cats, dead chickens, dead pigs, dead sheep, dead goats, dead rabbits, dead squirrels. I don't think we saw any dead cows, but almost everything else littered the roads, their innards churned out in ways that churned up my own innards. With hindsight this has always seemed to me to have been portentous of the horrific war in that region that was to follow years later.

When I had climbed into the cab back at the border I had noticed the stink of French cigarettes lurking and lingering in the atmosphere. I was so pleased to finally get a lift that I hadn't given it much thought. When I was at school one of the house masters used to smoke strong French cigarettes, they always made me nauseous. The driver, who was called Jacques, decided to light up, and the smooth smoke lingered around him for a while in that nonchalant way that implies quality, before casually sidling over towards my already distressed nostrils. To me the smell had slight faecal undertones, suggestive of a fat old tweed decked squire squatting on a one-legged hunting stool, catching his breath while lighting up, a monocle dripping out of one eye, slapping his knee with glee at the barbarism of his dogs.

To my relief this particular brand of French cigarette was not too strong, and though it made me feel a bit unwell, I accepted one when he offered it to me. My tobacco addiction had been reactivated back in Sicily by smoking joints. So when Jacques tossed me an unopened packet, I put it in my pocket it without comment.

When he first offered me the lift I was in a bit of an 'anywhere but here' mood, not really caring where he was going. It turned out that he was going to Athens, the capital of Greece, and it was going to take three days. This was partly due to the state of the roads. It was impossible to take a lorry at speed along such heavily damaged roads without wrecking the suspension or jangling the bones of the occupants till they dropped out. I had been to Romania with my mother and sister about six months earlier to visit my father's relatives, and I found that the whole vibe of this place was similar to that of Romania. There were pot-bellied women in black dresses, wearing black stockings and black head shawls as if in a permanent state of mourning. They waddled around on legs that suggested that they either had arthritis or had had too many babies. They paused every now and again, either to view with pride their familial domain or to catch their breath before moving on. Hens pecked around these old ladies who must have seemed like queens to them. Dogs lounged against walls as the day warmed up. A dusty cockerel flew awkwardly up onto a fence post, frizzing his feathers out and looking as if he had had a bad hair day, before preening himself back into shape. Damage to the mortar on their walls made the buildings look poverty stricken, as if the men worked such long hours during the day that they had no time for the niceties of life, or were so discouraged by their plight that they were no longer motivated to maintain the dignity of their own homes.

The day wore on and Jacques seemed content to drive without trying to communicate. It would probably have been too difficult to wave his hands around in sign language while avoiding the potholes in the road. I tried to get used to the French cigarettes he had given me, but I was smoking them more out of addiction than pleasure. When evening came we pulled up at the roadside, and Jacques set up a camping stove in the middle of the cab and began to cook supper for us. The first thing he did when we stopped was to leap out of the cab for a few minutes. I hadn't noticed at the time but he had returned with a bottle of wine. This had been cooling on the axle between the lorry and its trailer as we drove. Being French his cooking wasn't bad, and the wine was pleasant and certainly very conducive to drowsiness. The tell-tale question "Do you have a girlfriend?" never came, either in sign language or in any other form, and there was no attempt whatever on his part to solicit sex. So eventually I climbed into the bunk bed beneath his. Feeling a warm glow from the wine, and with a belly full of good food, I fell asleep. This routine continued for three days, and because conversation was in short supply I had plenty of time to think.

The similarities of this land to Romania caused my thoughts to frequently drift to my father. These were thoughts that didn't come naturally to me. My first instinct was always to avoid and bury the sadness that welled up when I thought about my loss. My father died very suddenly; he was fifty years old at the time, and I was ten. There had been no warning at all, the day before had been a perfectly normal day. To me at that age, death was something far away that happened to other people who weren't as lucky as I was. It wasn't even on my radar when it came crashing through the ceiling. I didn't even hear the sound of it coming. The suddenness of it left me stunned, a dust caked ghoul of a child sitting next to a pile of rubble. Our family was a pretty traditional family for those times. This was an age when mummy stayed home and looked after the children while daddy went out to work. For a child this was uncomplicated and secure. That was the norm for most people back then. While cracks were starting to appear because of the Sixties ethos that romanticised promiscuity, rebellion and irresponsibility – seeing these attitudes as somehow creative – the one parent family was still far from being a commonplace phenomenon. It still turned heads if the life of someone you knew did not follow the simple tried and tested domestic pattern of two parents plus children, in a married household.

After my father died, my mother took over his job as manager of the inner city catering complex that he had previously run. At that time, for a woman to do this was a very big deal. For a woman to be accepted in a managerial role merited an article in the local Nottingham newspaper. I like to think she was ahead of her time, but to me as a child she was completely neglectful. Even though we lived on the premises, the hours she worked meant we had no family life whatever. She slept until it was time to let the cleaners in at 7.00 am, then slept again till 9.00 am when she went to the office to begin work. After this the pubs and restaurants in the complex began to open and she divided her time between the office, the cellar, and the bars and restaurants. When the premises closed down for the afternoon she slept again for several hours, after which she went back to the office until things started to reopen at 6.00 pm. In the evening she tended to spend her time downstairs in the main restaurant as part of the public face of things. This went on late into the night. After closing time came the daily stock taking, which usually went on until after midnight.

It was as if somebody had suddenly turned the lights off and left me in the dark. But I soon realised that the darkness can be quite an exciting place. No one can see you in the dark, so no one can hold you to account. It was a gloomy, visceral infra-red thrill, a slender, lurid flickering flame the colour of liquid sewage. I was free to mould my own life as I saw fit. For an adolescent to be thinking like this was of course incendiary, but to me it held a kind of warmth. If I could not have the comforting hugs of a mother or a father, then I would generate my own comfort from within. I would create my own feel good factor.

My colourful imagination was perfectly capable of doing this, and in later years excessive sexual fantasies were the stopper for that emptiness which I was constantly and energetically dodging in any way that I could. I was far too rowdy and hyperactive as a youngster to sit quietly in the office with my mother and the other staff, doing drawings like my four-year-old sister. So I got shooed out and left to my own devices. As I grew further into adolescence belated attempts at affection by my mother made me feel uncomfortable and so I shunned them.

Those few things that did bear a resemblance to family life just sent me deeper into feelings of resentment because of the twisted forms that they took. For example, in the evening my sister and I were allowed to have a meal in one of the alcoves of the restaurant where, if she was not too busy, my mother would join us. I always preferred to be left alone to enjoy my steak, mushrooms and chips, burying myself in the delicious savoury flavours of the fried food.

Another desultory attempt at family life was Sundays.

Sunday always used to be a very quiet day, and by tradition a day off from work for most people. All the shops were closed on Sunday. To me the city had a melancholic feel to it. The church bells clanging away in the distance, their chimes scaring doves into flight as they danced in their lofty towers, playing with heavenly light and talking powerfully to the angels, their steel tongues bellowing glory as they swung to and fro, with skinny, diminutive men looking up in terror as they serviced the ropes.

We went to visit my father's grave every Sunday. Sometimes my mother wept, sometimes she just looked miserable. The taxi would wait for us in the graveyard car park. Then it would take us on to the riding stables, where my sister and I would go off to our different riding groups.

It was the mid-Sixties, and to an adolescent the fashionable philosophy of the time seemed like the perfect food. It directed me exactly to where I already wanted to go. Being so young I imbibed the thinking of the time rather than consciously assenting to it. It was energy, it was freedom, it was sex, it was youth, it was colour, it was music with a tribal rhythm, and it was hostile towards anything old and restrictive. I had no external influences to stop me sliding faster and faster down into this dark, smelly, slippery hole.

We crossed the border into Greece. The roads were certainly in a better state of repair than in Yugoslavia and we made much better progress towards our destination.

I noticed that the architecture had taken on a hint of an Eastern ambiance. As well as the pastel colours that one normally associates with hot countries, and the squat, sprawling, shallow roofed houses that speak of a drier climate, there were also more domed buildings than I was used to seeing. Most of these appeared to be religious in nature and were probably Greek Orthodox churches, but they reminded me more of mosques and synagogues than of churches. The English parish church with its gnarled stonework and hard edges could not have been more different. A peasant bringing in the sheaves in the slanting light of an autumn evening would not look out of place next to an English parish church. But here everything was more attuned to the goatherd with his flock of plonking bells and uncouth smells, winding his way down the cobblestones in the heat of the day, and avoiding eye contact with the priest who stood ominously at the entrance of the church.

Chapter 6

Bent Watches

After several days of travel, during which Jacques had been pleasant but uncommunicative company, we reached Athens at night. I was dropped off at some point in the city that had an industrial appearance. and I was immediately lost with no way of orientating myself. I had no clue which way to go to find a more friendly environment. There were long tall fences on either side of the road, as well as the harsh, florescent smells of chemicals that were as simplistic and unsubtle as the plastics with which they were associated. I began to traipse in the direction of the greatest light, towards what might have been a city centre. After about an hour of walking shops and parks started to appear, but everything was closed and the city was quiet. Eventually, feeling very tired and bottling my concerns about stray dogs, I made myself as comfortable as possible down a darkened alley. There I went to sleep snorting at the smell of rotting vegetables coming from the bins of a nearby café.

In the morning I scrounged some money from passers-by and had a much needed coffee. That first cuppa, whether it is tea or coffee, always puts a positive complexion on the day for me. At the time I would have been reluctant to admit how much my sense of well-being depended on this simple ritual. It always gave me the feeling that if all the world collapsed around me, at least I had my cuppa to fall back on. In the mornings I would often stare out of café windows and anticipate an ill-defined but positive future of infinite possibilities.

After a little consideration I realised that I needed to find the action, that place in every city that is given over to youth, partying, drunkenness and drugs. I didn't put it in quite those terms, but after asking a few people I was directed to an area called 'the Plaka', near to the Acropolis hill. On arrival it was instantly obvious that I had not been misdirected. It was an area of cafés and bars, many with outdoor seating. With striding backpackers arriving and looking around gleefully. Apart from a handful of over-thirty-fives there were no old people.

I desperately needed somewhere to stay. Being on the road had again left me with that disconnected feeling, like a balloon that has been abandoned to the air currents. I needed to tie myself down for a while for the sake of my own sanity. The Plaka had several hostels, or pensions as they were called in Greece. I found these were cheap, and that I would easily be able to finance my stay with begging. It was in one of these pensions that I met Fred and Sheila.

Fred and Sheila were British. He was a Cockney and she was half Greek. They sold cheap Rolex watches to anyone who was stupid enough to believe that such a thing existed. Many of those who bought them undoubtedly believed that they had been stolen. So one could argue that when the watch broke down a few weeks later, and they realised that they had been sold a cheap imitation, they had got what they deserved. Fred was a wiry, wily gutter rat who would not have seemed out of place in a Dickens novel. He had a goatee beard that looked as if he was imitating his mate the devil. When he spoke to you he glanced at you side on in a conspiratorial fashion, whisky eyes glinting with wicked gold. I don't know if he was part Gypsy, but to him everybody else was a 'mark', to be inveigled of their money. He did not have even a drop of sentimentality in his veins, and one wonders how it was possible for him and Sheila to have any sort of relationship at all since all he seemed to think about was his pragmatic criminality. Sheila said she had been a junkie once, addicted to heroin, and that she had managed to break the habit. If that was true then the fact that she was a little overweight now bore testimony to her claim to being clean, since junkies were nearly always skinny.

I thought I would try a bit of this wheeling and dealing myself. I have never been particularly drawn to criminality or dishonesty, and it was mainly due to my amorality that I considered this course of action rather than due to some sort of strongly ingrained urge to defraud others. In fact I was only vaguely aware that there was something wrong with these watches at this point in time. There was a thin Canadian girl, Lara, who joined us in our business endeavours. We simply went out onto the streets of the Plaka and approached people offering them cheap, high quality watches. I am not a natural salesman by any stretch of the imagination. My introverted personality means that I am not good at the banter that is so essential to convincing other people to buy something they do not really want. But these watches obviously caught people's interest; they did seem to sell themselves, albeit at quite a slow rate. However the money I made was comparable to that which I could make from straightforward begging, and begging was easier. So when I heard that Fred had been threatened by a customer whose watch had broken down prematurely, I decided that begging was probably a safer and more dependable way of making money. Eventually Fred, Sheila and Lara decided to resort to begging as well. There were plenty of tourists and well-off Americans to go round, so this was not a problem.

In the hostel we all slept in communal dormitories. The hostel was patronised mainly by backpackers. There was a spectrum of types. Most of those at the top end of the spectrum were American backpackers. They tended to have money in American Express accounts, and were often students or just young people looking for adventure, wanting to explore beyond their personal horizons and experience strange new cultures.

In the middle of the spectrum were a lot of Europeans, at various stages of hippification.

At the bottom were the homeless; drifting, hardened hippies like myself who considered themselves to have discarded any norms and ties connected with conventional society.

The common denominators that facilitated communication between us were youth, travel, adventure and drugs. Because of these there was a camaraderie between us, even if unity would have been too strong a word to use in this context.

For the naïve and green, hostels like this were the place to get your money and your passport stolen. If you had valuables, the best – in fact the only place to keep them safe – was on your person. Many used a pouch on a cord around their necks, or kept valuables pressed against some part of their bodies where contact, if disturbed, would be noticed. More than one trusting young innocent leapt gleefully into the murky waters of the backpacking travel scene, only to have their legs broken on the nefarious rocks that hid just below the surface. I never stole from anyone in the hostel and I don't think Fred or Sheila did either, though I can't be sure.

Chapter 7

Immaculate Perfection

She was pristine and immaculate, but in a beautiful sort of way, not like a fixed, plastic Barbie doll. In a woman the unblemished look can come over as very unreal, and to the more mature mind it can actually be a bit of a turn off. I was not of a mature mind and I was willing to take this relationship, if that is not too grandiose a term to describe what followed, as far as it would go.

She was married, she told me as we faced each other over the table in the small, crowded Greek café. During the conversation I discovered that she was rich and well connected, and it seemed she was slumming it. This was partly to see how the other half lived, and partly because she was bored and disillusioned with her own kind and wanted a bit of unrestrained adventure and unrestricted release. This suited me just fine. It was not difficult to believe the story about her background. I could easily imagine her slipping seamlessly through a huddle of royals at a party without ruffling any feathers. She spoke with an overly posh accent and somewhat condescendingly referred to me as 'boy', even though she herself was most likely only in her mid-twenties. While some of this was probably affected, and she seemed to fit the stereotype a bit too perfectly, I did not doubt the basic truthfulness of her description of herself and her life.

Once again the 'straight' problem had reared its ugly head, but nevertheless, I could not believe my luck. I had managed to capture this beautiful woman's interest without too much difficulty at all.

We eventually broke loose, drinking the cheap Retsina wine served in large jugs everywhere in Athens, and then running for it without paying. We both got very drunk and very silly. But once she had decided that she had had enough unrestricted release, she affected what I hoped was feigned boredom, after which she left, and I never saw her again. No doubt she found some other tomcat to lure into her orbit with her cream-draped personality.

Chapter 8

The Hermit Crab

Jeff was American, and he lived in a small van parked under the Acropolis that was barely big enough to sleep in. It was he who had supplied Fred and Sheila with the dodgy watches that we had sold in the nearby Plaka. He was notoriously grumpy and cynical, and was hostile towards any behaviour that was even faintly suggestive of pleasantness or cordiality. Kindness would be batted away forcefully, sympathy would be sunk instantly by a torpedo of sarcasm. When he spoke, his voice always seemed to seethe with the spitting acid of nastiness. He behaved like someone who felt he had been betrayed by his dearest dreams, and so was fully justified in striking out at anything or anyone that reminded him of those dreams. Lara, the skinny Canadian girl, seemed to be his girlfriend, and sometimes she played the role of being the only one who could understand this complex and deep feeling man. Because of my youth and naïvety a part of me believed there may well be something inscrutable about him, but even so I didn't ever feel the desire or need to socialise with him.

The strange thing was, one had the impression that he never left that small van of his on the hill, but lived forever within its steel shell, lurking like a hermit crab and snapping at anything that got too near to the entrance. The American war in Vietnam had recently finished, so he might have been a draft dodger. At the opposite end of the scale he might have been a veteran who had seen too much pain to believe any longer in the existence of any sort of goodness in this universe. I don't know which, if either of these he was, but I avoided him whenever possible. For all its faults the hippie philosophy was a positive one, and a hopeful one, even if most of this was drug addled and shot through with foolishness. We were searching for happiness; misery was a non-starter in our book.

More than once I drank with young American soldiers and sailors who seemed to be close to my own age. I am not sure if they were on their way home from the Vietnam conflict, which had officially ended about a year earlier. The war itself was rarely mentioned as we drank ouzo and smoked marijuana in the shadow of the Acropolis during the now warm nights. On one occasion someone told me that they had been involved in the shelling of the Vietnamese coast, but he gave no details. On another occasion I was told there was a nuclear submarine parked in the nearby harbour capable of destroying the world several times over.

I knew I was a bit of a social limpet in this situation, and made no pretensions of being anything else. I listened more than spoke when I was in their company. I do not recall meeting any who were traumatised, None of them dove under tables at the first loud noise; nobody had a face that was knotted with anxiety or eyes that were fixed like nails on some point beyond death. Most seemed quite normal. The groups I sat with were neither particularly open nor particularly closed off, and they let me sit with them without shunning me in any way.

Like most men I was curious about war, despite my pacifistic philosophy. Like most men I wondered how I would react under fire. I could not imagine myself running towards a machine gun spitting red hot bullets at a rate that could cut me in two, or tramping through a jungle knowing that each step could potentially set off a man trap that would impale me on a spike adorned frame, leaving me jabbering with shock till the lights went out in my sightless far-seeing eyes. I did not want to believe that I was a coward, I did not want to go there in my thinking, but deep down I was sure that I was, and that I could never do those things myself.

Chapter 9

And Again

On one occasion I went up to look at the Acropolis, and it didn't do a great deal for me.

Greek philosophers, Druids and Buddhist monks are all different creatures. I had never been attracted to the chalkiness of Greek philosophy; it was too well defined and intellectual, too black and white, too much about cold concepts and living in ivory towers, detached from the potential warmth and colour of the real world. It smacked of formality, discipline and learning by rote, with no tangible end game. It was all about clambering endlessly through scaffolds of abstraction with very little contact with real experience. It seemed to suggest that it was erudite to be left with a profound sense of emptiness and uncertainty. In that respect it was similar to Buddhism. At that time I sensed rather than understood these things, and so my feelings directed me away from classical Greek culture. I seemed to know that this road came to a dead end without even starting along it.

Things were starting to become staid, repetitive and boring again. I had my small group of arm's length friends, but so what? The weather was warming up, and I had seen and experienced all I wanted to of Athens and the Plaka youth scene.

However when I started to talk about leaving I was surprised to notice that there were small peevish suggestions of disloyalty coming from Fred, Sheila and Lara. This should have moved me, since they clearly saw me as belonging to their group. But to me it was just water off a duck's back. I wasn't about to let sentimentality keep me from continuing forwards on my great adventure. I was still riding wild horses and chasing the sunset. Their lives were far too tiny for me, and far too tame.

So I picked up my sleeping bag and left.

Lara came with me to the invisible edge of the Plaka region. I asked her to come with me but she declined, apparently preferring the company of grumpy old Jeff holed up in his little van on the Acropolis hill. She gave me a platonic kiss, which I regarded as pretty useless, and had trouble figuring out exactly what it meant. Then, without further ado, and with the polite applause of Plato's ghost ringing in my ears, I left Athens.

My journey north was less eventful than my journey south. I eventually picked up a lift from a couple of French guys who were obviously drug culture types, but presented a harder demeanour than most others I had met who referred to themselves hippies. The French pair had short hair and wore denim jackets without badges or patches, giving them the look of American Vietnam veterans. There was something businesslike about them; this combined seamlessly with the general aloofness that I had come to associate with most French people. They were taciturn in their dealings with me, frequently speaking French to each other in a way that to me in the back seat sounded very much like mockery and disdain. The occasional slight turn of a head in my direction when they laughed didn't help. Insecure as I was, with virtually no inner defences against criticism, my anxiety increased. I clearly wasn't making it as a hippie. These guys weren't full on hippies but they had plenty of 'cool' about them. They seemed in control, exuding bravado. And so, feeling somewhat pathetic, while not wanting to and in a way that was almost uncontrollable, I looked up to them for approval. I would have been red meat for any cult that I might have stumbled across in my meanderings Eastwards.

They were heading for Istanbul, the doorway to Asia, with me in tow. I was unwilling to let go. Everything was flapping in the hot air blowing in through the car window.

Chapter 10

Nirvana

In those days I imagined myself to have spirit guides. They were in the form of profound ascended individuals such as Buddha, or yogis who had achieved Nirvana. I believed that they spoke to spiritually attuned individuals through feelings and guiding urges of the heart. This was supposedly to give meaningful direction to people's lives, and so to bring them into the ultimate bliss of Nirvana. The goal was to become infinite, and so to experience everything that was, and is, and will be, all at once. I visualised Nirvana as a boiling river of flowers, beautiful animals and shapes, and as pleasures that were infinite and beyond proportions. I believed that, in the universe, every possible parallel universe existed, as well as every impossible parallel universe. And that in the state of Nirvana, outside of time and space, you experienced everything in all of them, all at once.

Effectively, when you achieved Nirvana – you became God.

Chapter 11

A Dog Called Yogi

We reached Istanbul to the sound of the call to prayer. This was my first real taste of the flavours of the East, and my ears drank in the exotic strangeness of these sounds as they echoed back and forth across the city. I had only ever heard this sort of thing on corny old black and white movies depicting North Africa against a backdrop of deserts, empire and war. They had characters that were so flat, as to be nothing but caricatures. The central protagonists all speaking in their clipped upper class English accents, while the skinny, dark skinned local always spoke in a wibbly-wobbly form of pidgin English. Often a native would scamper after the white man, snivelling sycophantically for the sake of a few coins; these were usually thrown to the ground forcing him to dive to the dirt to retrieve them. Sometimes a shady, cloaked figure would surreptitiously emerge from a dark alley and stab some hapless victim in the back before making off with his bag of silver.

The warbling sounds of prayer seemed to express a longing, maybe even a desperation for something more. These ended gracefully, with all the cries from across the Bosphorus waters landing and folding their wings quietly to wait for the next time they were needed.

The giant domes of the mosques were low slung and crouching compared with Western cathedrals. They resembled the shells of sea creatures, and their thin minarets stabbed the sky above. From these towers the criers spread their voices far and wide.

In modern times loudspeakers are usually used, spoiling the sound somewhat with their tell-tale blare.

Unlike the movies, there were cars and electricity here, and a few modern shop fronts. The streets were very narrow, tending to be pedestrian, and the buildings on either side were often five storeys tall, enclosing the continuous ooze of people traffic below.

The indoor markets did not disappoint, they had a genuine Eastern feel to them. The tackiness of the tourist trade had not yet taken hold in Istanbul. Set in arched corridors, the markets were a riotous galaxy of shape and colour. The craftsmanship that had gone into some of these items was stunning. It seemed mildly tragic that such lovely artefacts should be so eclipsed by so many of their peers vying for attention. My head didn't know which way to turn. No sooner had I caught sight of one of these wonders than my eyes were immediately pulled away by another. There were stained glass lanterns that spoke magic from within sensuously bent filigree, skilfully carved furniture that looked immovable as it squatted sturdily displaying its glinting brass appendages and inlaid stonework, rivers of colourful clothing cascading down from the ceiling, substantial candles that were probably scented, spices in ancient-looking wooden display boxes, sweets that were alien both in their constituents and in their appearance, plates and pottery with patterns and shapes that must have drained every possible dreg from the bowl of human imagination, and of course avalanches of carpets that were fit to be graced by the noble toes of the mightiest of kings. All these things drawing people's attention away from their purses and wallets, giving the skinny pick-pocket weaving like a needle through the crowd a very profitable day.

Even though I loved the colours and the shapes I didn't enjoy the press of the crowd and I was glad to escape at the other end.

In many of the cities along what was then called 'The Hippie Trail' there were well known focal points for western travellers to gather. In Istanbul, one of these was a milk bar at which backpackers frequently congregated to socialise, drink coffee and exchange stories. People were travelling in both directions, with those returning from further east looking thinner, dustier and somewhat gaunt. To my eyes they looked as if they had acquired some sort of tough, wiry wisdom from their experience. Then there were those heading out towards Asia, who were generally cleaner looking, happier and better dressed.

The out-goers were bright eyed and keen, raring to go, whereas the returners always had a bit of a laid-back, world-weary slouch to them. This was not entirely show, but it did say 'Look at me, I'm really cool now'. Many of the returners were dressed in the thin flannel clothes worn by a lot of people out East. They always resembled pyjamas, some even had stripes on them. They were designed to keep people cool in the oppressive heat of Asia.

I had already parted ways with the two French lads who had given me a lift, and after a short search I found a building site containing an incomplete house. There were no fences to scale and no security guards evident, so I went into the house, unrolled my sleeping bag on the dusty concrete floor, and used it as a rudimentary doss. The windows and doors were not yet fitted and there were trowels and other building paraphernalia lying around. I never saw builders, so I don't know if it was an abandoned project, or maybe things had been put on hold for financial reasons.

It provided me with a faint but welcome sense of security at night.

After getting up in the mornings I would beg money from the wealthier looking Western travellers, and then go to drink coffee at the milk bar. There was not much for me to do. I had no great interest in sightseeing so I spent long periods of time looking out of the café window and feeling bored. I had only just arrived but I was getting depressed again.

There was a strip of lawn and paved public park that extended the length of the avenue just outside the milk bar. I would stroll along this sometimes and sit at the other end on a bench facing some sort of cenotaph. The cenotaph had writing on it with strange curly accents that reminded me of fishing hooks and claws. Such focal points have an attraction for the emotionally unfocused like myself. While sitting there I was approached by one of the ubiquitous stray dogs so common all over Asia. His companions ignored me and lay scattered around overheating in the sun. But he seemed to want attention so I petted him, blissfully unaware of the danger from rabies and a thousand other disgusting and life threatening ailments that he might be carrying. I felt I had clicked with this dog in a special way, so I decided to name him. I cast around in my mind for something appropriate to call him. If he had a breed I didn't know what it was. The chances were that he was some kind of mongrel. He showed a strong interest in people so he may have been a pet at one time before being tossed out onto the street. He was a medium sized dog, about the size of a border collie but much stouter than that breed. His coat was too thick for the climate he found himself in.

As I petted him he had a distant look in his eyes, not fully responding to the affection I was showing him. In the end the only name I could think of was 'Yogi'. So that was what, and how, I called him. Whenever I went to the park I would call him enthusiastically by his new name and he would approach me, slowly wagging his tail as though it was compulsory to do so.

It was about then that I started to dream about a coastal existence, palm trees swinging in the breeze, white sands, bare toes sinking innocently into sand and leaving playful footprints, and the laughter of the bright, sparkling, splashing waves. I figured Yogi would enjoy that sort of existence as well. He was obviously a city dog and I imagined the joy and bewilderment he would feel at suddenly finding himself on a deserted beach with plenty of washed-up fish to scavenge, and lots of shady foliage to doze under. Suddenly I was on a mission to rescue Yogi from his sorry life as a bedraggled city stray who picked at bins. I wanted him to experience paradise, to enjoy a houndly heaven on earth. I had in mind to travel to the south coast of Turkey, where I had heard the beaches were really nice. By now the weather was warm enough for sleeping out, so moving down there could be a really fabulous experience.

One night I went to see if I could find Yogi. Despite the bond I felt with him he did not follow me around, but stuck with his own kind. They tended to sleep around the cenotaph which was some way from any streetlights. It was not possible to see the dogs at night unless you strained your eyes, then you could pick out a few dark humps on the paving around the monument. None of the dogs could be described as big, but there were about fifteen of them. They were very quiet, and I hadn't noticed their presence when I went to call for Yogi. Inching forwards in the dark I shouted his name. All of a sudden there erupted a cacophony of noise, yelping, barking, growling or snarling depending on pack status. I was caught completely by surprise as dark shapes stood up. Some lunged towards me and stopped, while others, stiff legged, marched me off the property. I knew better than to turn my back on them and run, so I backed away cautiously. They were obviously streetwise, pragmatic dogs who knew better than pick a fight with a human. As soon as I had passed over some invisible threshold they calmed down and slumped back into their resting places hoping for a quiet night. Unbitten, but somewhat shaken, I left them in peace.

I didn't do that again.

I bumped into the French guys who had given me a lift to Istanbul and it just happened that they were going down to the south coast with similar ideas to myself. They agreed to give me a lift again. I told them about Yogi and asked if I could bring him along too. They discussed this between themselves in French, and as usual their speech had that grandiose 'hoity toity' sound to it, even more so when they started laughing. After a few moments of discourse they turned to me and agreed to take the dog as well. So later that day I set out with a piece of rope that I had found lying around on the building site, and after creating a simple choke lead, I called Yogi over. He came to me with no problem, and even though the lead seemed to make him a bit tense he soon accepted it and followed me along the road. He did not pull back, and apart from one or two dogs who raised their heads, the rest of the pack ignored our departure.

We met Albert and Julien, the French guys, at their car, and we were quickly bundled into the back while they both sat in the front. Then, with an obvious flourish of excitement from Albert and Julien, we were off. It was warm in the back of the car and it didn't take me long to get sweaty and sticky. Yogi was at my feet keeping very quiet; he was behaving like a dog who had accepted his lot, whatever that might be. Was he going to be fed or was he going to be put down? Or maybe both, he didn't know. He turned his head slowly and looked up at me. He wasn't going to argue, he'd have to take his chances, for better or worse.

We started to cross one of the Bosphorus bridges. It was a large, magnificent suspension bridge that spanned the Bosphorus Straits. As we passed the centre line Albert and Julien let out a whooping cheer. Yogi's head popped up, and I was baffled. They looked back, at me and when they noticed my confusion they explained that we had just crossed the mid-line of the bridge and we were now in Asia.

Finally we were worthy of the title of 'Travellers', and all the cred points that come with that title. We were intrepids facing down and leaning into the dust storm of unknown adventure. Unwilling, unable to turn back as we squared our jaws for what was to come.

Then Yogi was sick.

At this point I thought my lift was over, or at least that Yogi would have to be re-abandoned to the street. I was reluctant to do this in an area that was so new to him. On this side of the bridge he didn't have a pack, and there was little or no chance that he would find his way back to the cenotaph. To my surprise the French guys were very understanding, and they themselves cleaned out the vomit from the floor in the back and allowed us back into the car.

We continued east and then south. Yogi puked twice more, and I hated watching the regret creeping into Albert and Julien as they reassessed the wisdom of their kindness. By the time we got to the south coast Yogi and I were holding on by our fingertips, and we almost turfed ourselves out of the car when we got there. We were relieved to be free of the ominous atmosphere that had built up like a thunder-faced giant in the confined space of the vehicle.

I encouraged Yogi to stay with me; he did not do this on his own initiative. I needed to call hard and slap my thighs till they were red to make him follow me. Sometimes he sat in front of random tourists begging scraps and completely ignoring me. I could have persevered, and I might have ended up with the dog of my dreams, loyal, affectionate, protective, sensitive and all those other doggy qualities that we so much love and admire. But it seemed too much like hard work, spontaneous love wasn't this dog's forte. I took him to the beach and my last memory of him was his furry backside undulating off along the beach without so much as a yelp of thank you from the other end. All the soppy movies I had ever watched involving dogs and kangaroos and dolphins (notably no cats) rescuing their owners from certain death came crashing down mightily that day. I never saw him again.

Chapter 12

The Italian Rob

I was in a small seaside village called Side (pronounced 'Sida') which had orientated itself towards tourism for its income. It benefited from an ancient Roman amphitheatre as well as other extensive ruins, some of which were very overgrown. Between the ruins and the sea was a large collection of ramshackle wooden huts. These were all empty, their doors flapping in any breeze that happened to grace the coastline at this time of year. They were used by the Turks in the height of summer during the holiday season. But right now they seemed to be ownerless, there was nothing in them to identify any sort of possession.

One could almost say that they were badly made by design as they were constructed of bare planks, and any wind blowing through the gaps between them would cool the occupants during the sweltering summer weather.

But for now they were the fulfilment of any Tarzanic dreams I might still be harbouring. If I wasn't going to make it to the Amazon, swinging around on vines and dodging native blow darts, then this would have to do.

Several of these shacks were in the form of covered platforms, looking out to sea from their perches on top of the ancient walls. Tarzans would have loved it here, likewise Jane.

It was about then that I met the Italian hippies. They must have arrived in Side at about the same time as me because we all moved into one of these premier beach accommodations together. They had a slick, greasy look to them that reminded me of olives; it was as if sweat was a fashion statement amongst them. They all had straight, black hair, except for Niccolo who had a full mane of long curly ginger hair, and was openly gay.

In those days homosexuals often gravitated towards the sexual liberalism of the hippie scene. In their thinking it was one of the few places they could find acceptance, since hippie thinking – or not thinking, as the case may be – tended to deliberately dynamite any established social norms in the name of freedom of thought and unrestrained creativity. Nice in theory, but in practice it just left you with a pile of rubble.

There were four of them in total: Niccolo, Tommaso, Lorenzo and Francesco.

Tommaso's hair was short. He was tubby and wore circular spectacles which did nothing to make him look in vogue and Sixties, but rather gave him a demented schoolboy look. Somehow his sporadic black stubble contributed to this. Lorenzo was slim and had long, slick hair that slid down to his waist and shone vampirically glossy, with sharp pointed ends. This, along with his death's head belt buckle, made him look a little dangerous. Finally there was Francesco, who seemed to be their leader. Like all leaders he hid his emotions, presenting a calm, competent front. Some things seem to be a common denominator in all human interactions, and the 'leader face' is just one of those things.

Noticing how all their names ended in 'o' I considered calling myself Stuarto, but decided against it. They were tolerant of my presence even though there was already a dynamic to their group. It seemed as though they already knew each other from Italy. Communication was not a problem. Niccolo could speak good English, and the rest of them had at least a smattering of English.

In the evening we smoked marijuana from a chillum, sitting cross legged and sharing it around as if we were a mystic brotherhood. At each puff a fleece of smoke would linger and then slowly disperse, only to be replaced by another before it was completely gone. Conversation was sporadic and brief as we absorbed our surroundings and postured in glassy eyed meditation, hoping that we looked erudite and profound, perhaps with a deep Cosmic glint in the pupils of our eyes.

We slept on our raised platform that resembled a tree house, ascending and descending by a set of wooden steps that led down one side of the structure. We could hear the Mediterranean sloshing languidly against the beach, and felt safe in our fragile fortress.

In the mornings I would go to the amphitheatre and wait for busloads of tourists to arrive. These were usually Americans or Germans, both of whom seemed loud and brash as well as physically large in height and girth. Both nationalities wore tasteless Hawaiian style shirts, garishly slashed with flowers, palm trees and parrots, as if somebody was trying to take revenge on the snooty and exclusive world of in vogue fashion and art. I am not loud or brash myself, so that side of the German temperament has always baffled me a bit. This could be due to my father's family coming from a breakaway ethnic group of Germans, possibly resulting in his people taking a more laid-back attitude towards life.

When begging, I would instinctively target those who didn't swagger too much, and then ask them for money. I would use this money to buy a large bowl of yogurt and a loaf of bread from the local shop.

Then I sometimes went to explore the rubble and scrubland behind the ancient walls. I would skip from stone to stone with the grace and accuracy of a fairy. There was no danger of turning my ankle over; physically I was still energetic, and mentally I was still attuned enough to hit my target. When I did this I was unaware of the danger of snakes. I didn't realise this was the ideal environment for snakes to sun themselves on the secluded boulders, and then slip away into the dark gaps to hunt. However I didn't see a single snake as I leapt around exploring this mysterious hidden world.

One day we decided to visit Antalya. Three of us hitch-hiked as a group, and we soon got a lift from a local Turkish lorry. Like most small lorries in the East, it seemed to shuffle and snuffle along. The cab was already full of people. There were two other men as well as the driver and a teenage boy of about fourteen. We squeezed in uncomfortably and a bit too intimately, and then we set off. It wasn't long before the man pressed up against me started to grope my thigh. I was by now very experienced in dealing with situations like this. I politely removed his hand and shook my head. After a couple more tries he gave up. Niccolo however was being solicited by the teenage boy and appeared to be enjoying it. What surprised me was how normal this behaviour was deemed by these men, in such a morally stringent country as Turkey.

We had quite an interesting day in Antalya exploring and sitting in cafés. Then we went back to Side.

The main shop in Side was little more than a local grocery store, and didn't appear to have expanded yet in response to the influx of tourism. Many of their wares sat outside the shop on the small road leading down to the beach, and were vulnerable to shoplifting. I personally had few qualms about that sort of behaviour. I viewed large and medium sized businesses as the enemy of the people, and I had no problem stealing from them. But I was not a thief by nature. On an earlier adventure, at the age of seventeen, when I travelled to St Ives, I fell in with some youngsters who were a motley and troublesome crew. One of them was on the run from a 'care home' and the others, both male and female, about my age, were all emotionally confused or distressed in one way or another. They were, roughly speaking, hippies. We slept on top of a pile of deck chairs packed under an alcove and secured by a tarpaulin, that were awaiting the holiday season. This was a good spot, as it kept us both safe and relatively warm. You had to climb up the substantial pile of chairs before gaining access to the top, which was just below the alcove ceiling.

Sometimes we would go out and roam the narrow streets at night. One night another lad and I found an unlocked car parked near the jetty. We climbed in and sat in the front seats. Neither of us could drive and we made no attempt to steal the car, instead we saw it as a place of warmth from the chill which was now building up outside. We saw ourselves as borrowing rather than stealing the use of vehicle, and we reasoned that since it had been left open, the owner obviously didn't mind people sitting in it at night. I searched the glove compartment and found some cigarettes. We started to smoke these, and we stretched our reasoning about the vehicle being open to include justification for smoking this person's cigarettes, while all the time ignoring the pitiful screams of protest coming from our consciences. I cleaned the inside of the car windows as payment, in an attempt to quieten this inner voice a bit.

Perhaps the worst thefts I was involved in were those times when we went shoplifting as a group in the local supermarket. In my mind this counted as a medium sized business that had no right stripping people of their hard-earned cash. To me such a business could easily absorb the cost of our theft. I believed we had a right to claw back some of their profit for the sake of the ordinary people. With hindsight I would say that it was probably a small business and it might have suffered financial distress as a result of our dishonest activity. This was in the days before security cameras were in every corner of every shop, and in every bus and every street. The tightest security this supermarket had was a wide angle mirror in one corner of the ceiling. We would fill our shopping bags with goods and buy a bar of chocolate from the schoolgirl who manned the till, then we would walk out carrying our heavy loads, apparently unseen by this single member of staff. Maybe she sympathised with our actions in some temperamental adolescent way, or maybe she was too dumb and unobservant to notice what we were doing. Or possibly she might have been too scared to raise the alarm. I don't know which of these it was, but we always got away with it, we were never challenged.

Strange as it may seem, in view of my behaviour at this time, as I have already said, I was not a thief by nature. For me, stealing never had a compulsive element to it, I was never addicted to it, I never identified with it, and I never truly enjoyed it. I always preferred face to face begging rather than more nefarious methods of acquisition. This was where I parted ways with my Italian friends. They had no qualms about stealing from the sort of small business at which I bought my yogurt. Because of this, it was not long before conflict arose between them and the local people, and not long after that till the Turkish police became involved. Socially I may have been a fool, morally I may have been bankrupt, but there was absolutely nothing wrong with my survival instincts. My alarm bells started ringing loudly immediately I heard that the police were taking an interest. At that time the Turkish police were about as far from the friendly English village bobby as you can get. In fact you could say that they were the antithesis of what a British person would have expected from the law. They were thugs who wore their uniforms untidily, jackets as if ripped open at the neck, stubble and sweat giving them an unclean appearance, walking with a slouching stoop that somehow resembled a cruel claw and having a reputation for indiscreet brutality. With their beaky mouths and gangly postures one could not help but be reminded of goblins. When I heard that Niccolo had been arrested I immediately avoided the beach hut for fear of becoming associated with their activities. I knew that innocence and guilt did not even come onto the radar as far as the local police were concerned, rape and beatings were more in vogue in their realm of activity. It was possible for a Westerner to disappear without a trace, and if anyone even cared enough to make enquires they would be met with shrugs and silence. I was not about to let myself be trapped because of someone else's stupidity.

Niccolo was however freed and allowed to return to the beach hut, but from the tone of their conversation, and Niccolo's generally distressed demeanour, I concluded that some abuse must have been involved during his arrest, and I decided to leave as soon as possible. Which as it turned out was immediately. I won't say that it didn't trouble me to jump from this sinking ship so promptly, especially while the others were gathering around Niccolo supportively, showing him solidarity.

But to linger in this situation, taking on the attitude of a martyr seemed to me like madness. Especially as there was nothing stopping any of them, including Niccolo, from also doing the sensible thing, and running for their lives.

Chapter 13

A Thoroughly Modern Turk

I headed North again, aiming for Ankara, the capital of Turkey. I was out in open country, mostly scrubland. Dust and heat were becoming the norm now, and the temperature was oppressive. I trudged along the road, with the heat shimmer disturbingly reminiscent of a flame about to ignite. A small lorry passed me, slowed a bit, and then sped up again. Two large mastiff dogs were trudging in my direction on the opposite side of the road. They were short haired and their skin sagged and hung on their tall frames. Like all mastiffs they had a sorrowful look to their faces, with constantly drooling jowls and weak, weary eyes. They stopped and looked me over from the other side of the road. Just then a local lorry pulled up. I climbed into the cab gratefully. As we pulled away I wondered idly about what such large dogs eat when they end up as strays. The Turks in this lorry were friendly and cheerful and I had none of the problems I had experienced on the lift to Antalya. After several lifts both long and short I found myself in Ankara. Cities have never been my thing, so Ankara was just a way station as far as I was concerned, not a destination. I intended to get vaccinated against various nasty diseases that I had heard about while I was *en route*. I was told that there was a free vaccination program in Ankara so I sought it out and got my jabs. I do not recall what these jabs were for, but without doubt they contributed to my body's defences when I later continued on my way.

While in Ankara I tended to use the cafés as emotional focal spots to rid myself once again of that awful lost feeling that haunts you when you are homeless. Turkish tea is drunk from little glasses that curve inward in the middle, called *ince belli*, which means literally 'slim-waisted'. It is normally made strong and without milk, but sweetened with cubes of sugar. Turkish cafés are pleasant places to be, usually with some outdoor seating, and with a communal feel to them. They hold the social niche occupied by pubs in the West.

Local people go to cafés to socialise and meet friends. In most cafés there is a corner where the chairs are worn smooth, that is permanently occupied by a gaggle of old men quietly playing board games and drinking tea with stalwart expressions on their faces. They always look a bit as if they are waiting for something, a train maybe.

It was in such a café that I got talking to Deniz and his friends. He was a young Turk of about seventeen whose one role model and prime hero was Ataturk, the early 20th century moderniser of Turkey. To him I seemed to represent in some way the values that he himself was aspiring towards. I had not heard of Ataturk until this point. Deniz's general attitude towards me was very similar to that of Andrea in Sicily. He expressed a naïve almost sycophantic admiration for all things Western and modern. As far as he was concerned the sooner Turkey became fully secularised the better. Turkey had recently done away with most of its Islamic culture, but still contained significant fundamentalist influences in some parts of the country. Deniz's attitude towards religion was similar to the attitudes held by most extreme left wingers. He regarded religion as a sort of social appendix, a useless leftover from a necessary but delusional stage of evolution, involved in the development of abstract thought and collaborative interaction. He had all the zeal of a radical, and I don't doubt that in future years he was involved in active, if not extreme, promotion of his beliefs. I was put on show to his friends, led around proudly like a prize bull, and presented as his Western friend. He took me to his home and, deftly avoiding his parents, showed me his bedroom. He had pictures of Ataturk on the walls, and various posters of rock bands including of course the ubiquitous Beatles. There was other stuff as well that appeared to have political undertones, but most of this was in Turkish, and apart from a few images that were obviously revolutionary in nature, I didn't understand any of it. At one point he decided to translate a speech by Ataturk for me. He obviously found this speech very stirring, and I tried not to look bored as his eyes teared up and the spittle of zeal flew involuntarily from his mouth.

He managed to convince an older friend of his to put me up for a few days. I soon got bored and restless as I realised that what I was looking for was not here. Certainly the dry bones of Deniz's politics (what I understood of it) did not inspire me one bit. Once again I was compelled and driven along by that obsessive voice that made me so aware of the emptiness and my inner need. I had not found a home here, nor had I expected to. A bunch of heavily politicised Turkish lads was not my idea of a community. And besides, they were straight, their style of dress was about as conventional as you could get. What really twisted my nose was that they couldn't even flavour it with something from their own culture. The conventions they were following were those of the West. To me this seemed as if they were somewhat tragically aping the West. They did not even have the self respect to contribute anything of their own to this style of dress. So, with more than a little disdain, I left these cultural simpletons, and carried on further East.

Chapter 14

The Night of the Wolf

Soon the route I was travelling started to look truly barren. It was once again hot and dust blown. Much of it was open hilly land with dry grass, scrub and sandy rock. The air had a constant reddish tint, and there was the occasional village that looked small enough to contain but a single family. I was hurrying to get through this land to somewhere with mountains, water and a cool breeze. I knew this part of Turkey had a reputation for being dangerous, especially for Westerners, and the sooner I got through it the better. I had a lift from a Turkish car driver who was heading East. His English was not good enough for conversation so I spent most of the lift taking in the desultory scenery which was gradually becoming more and more depressing.

It was getting dark and I was beginning to doze a bit.

Suddenly an animal loped across the headlights.

From the driver's excited reaction I knew it wasn't a stray dog. He threw one hand into the air in exclamation, and kept emphatically repeating a single word. He was speaking in Turkish but I knew what he was saying. It was obvious to me that we had just seen a wolf.

We reached a town at dusk, and he dropped me off on the outskirts. I could see a few residential tower blocks not far away. They poked up incongruously from the flat, barren ground. There were mounds of rubbish and earth along the side of the road, and the air was tinged an ever deepening red by the setting sun. I could not help but be reminded of the nightmarish descriptions of the post-apocalyptic earth that we all genuinely believed was inevitable. In those days such imagery was not the stuff of sci-fi thrillers that you could watch cosily from your armchair on Christmas day while happily munching mince pies. Back then such thoughts were terrifying, and you tried to avoid dwelling on them whenever possible. Ironically this town might have fared well in a nuclear war since it was out of the way and of no consequence to anyone, either militarily or economically.

The silhouettes of a few dark figures looked down on me from the mounds as I walked by. I was afraid since I knew this part of the country had a reputation for violence. I kept my eyes on the ground and carried on walking. Nothing happened, they just stood there as if transfixed to the spot by the hellish light behind them. They seemed like a kind of warning sign: 'carry on at your own peril', as their heads imperceptibly rotated to follow my progress. I moved towards the block of flats since there seemed to be nothing else to go towards, and since a plan was starting to form in my mind. Flats normally have basements and boiler rooms, and I knew from experience that the steps that led down to these could be good places to sleep undisturbed, even though the doors at the bottom were normally locked. On arriving at these surreal protrusions rising from the sandy ground, I realised that I was afraid to go inside in case I got trapped and beaten up or killed. The alternative was to sleep outside, but I was afraid of wolves and stray dogs. In the end I opted for a compromise. I slept down a small flight of steps outside one of the blocks of flats. I don't think I was reasoning very well at this point in time because when I did bed down, I realised that I was vulnerable to both wolves and men. If I slept at all that night it was in that twilight zone between wakefulness and sleep; the nervous part of me constantly listening for the sound of approach and watching for that shadow across my closed eyelids. I got up early in the morning and looked cautiously out of my depression at the bottom of the steps. Nobody was about, it was early. I took the chance to head straight for the road, and began to walk away from this dismal place, hoping a car would come along soon. The heat shimmer made it difficult to see exactly what was ahead, thus I felt as if I was heading towards nothingness, or maybe even something less than nothingness. The vision of some cool fresh green place beyond drew me forward.

After about an hour of walking, a fast moving plush looking car swerved to a halt in a way that made me suspicious. If this road had any legal speed limits they certainly were not enforced. The local police were probably too lazy to bother with something as adrenaline fuelled as a car chase, and besides I doubt any of their vehicles would have been up to it. Chances were that they had nothing more than a flea bitten donkey between them. This car spoke of money, which was explained by the fact that the driver was Iranian. As I got in another similar car swished past, slowing a little in the distance, and then speeding up again. Iran was much wealthier than Turkey. Some of its cities were modern and full of tall buildings that shone painfully in the burning glory of the midday sun. Iran was trying to be a modern state, as was Turkey, but at this point in history it was having much more success than Turkey.

It was a nice feeling to be tonning it along these straight dusty roads, apart from a slight unease at the fact that they were not in a brilliant state of repair. My driver however seemed to be adept at anticipating potholes and dodging them, or maybe flying over them. I wasn't really watching. Once again I was with someone whose English was next to nil, so much of the journey was spent looking out at the barren scenery flying past. The driver was well dressed in European style clothing. He was obviously trying to mimic the Western trendy style. This seemed to be the default position for Easterners who wanted to be modern. He pulled it off well, and would probably have been allowed into any London nightclub.

We shot through small villages with very little reduction in our speed. The driver seemed keen to get through this part of Turkey as quickly as possible, clearly aware that his opulence would attract attention from the poor locals, like a carcass would attract attention from carrion fowl. He was right – as we flew through one village at a speed that barely acknowledged its existence, a black robe with sleeve flapping caught the corner of my eye. Someone – who seemed to be female, though I can't say why – was doing an over arm bowl from the side of the road. Something sprayed across the road and the driver swerved instinctively. Nothing happened. He slowed a bit, looked in the mirror and sped up again. Someone had tried to crash us; a bottle had been thrown into the road. It could have been an angry mother who had lost a child to similar speeding cars, but it was more likely that there were menfolk hiding somewhere along the roadside to mug and rob us if we crashed, or stopped. That would have been a death sentence had we been seriously injured. We would have become food for vultures, and the car, even damaged, would have been a treasure chest for those people for several years to come.

When we got near to the Turkey-Iran border we came across a long queue of articulated lorries. To have so many hi-tech vehicles lined up in a row on a road that was barely a raised dirt track seemed incongruous. Many appeared to be European in origin and must have been in transit to wealthy Iran.

Despite their technology and power some of these lorries had fallen prey to mishaps. They had slid down the substantial bank on which the road was raised. They sat at precarious angles with their loads twisted out painfully like disjointed knees. I felt a little aghast at the predicament of these drivers. They were in big trouble. The cost to any company of the loss of a lorry had to be massive. If the drivers decided to stick with the vehicles until help came, they themselves would be in danger from the locals, who would have been able to spot their vulnerability from afar and home in on it like a pack of hyenas. These lorries were probably beyond saving, since it would have taken heavy lifting gear such as cranes to get them back up the bank. In some cases even disconnecting the cab would have been impossible because of how the coupling with the load had become twisted. The drivers must have gone home, their heads hung in shame at the inevitable rebuke and possible sacking that awaited them.

We passed the long queue on the other side of the narrow road without meeting any oncoming traffic, and arrived at the border post.

I parted ways with my Iranian lift and stood looking at the border post. It reminded me of a small military fort. It was obviously not up to all the commercial traffic it was getting but, very slowly, lorries from both sides were being let through. No doubt much of this was happening at an unofficial cost to the haulage companies that ran the lorries.

I had heard horror stories about such border posts. One involved a van load of Western hippies who were carrying drugs. As I understand it the quantity was not large, just enough for personal use and perhaps a bit more. When these drugs were discovered, the youngsters in the van were simply taken behind the border post and shot, without trial, delay or ceremony.

They will have joined the many other young travellers who simply evaporated while on the hippie trail. Their parents and relatives, having no idea what happened, will gradually, monotonously, have lost a little more hope with each passing year. Thinking about this, I realised how sensible my rule of not carrying drugs while travelling actually was.

I went into the quadrangle through the main gate. I felt trapped in a kind of lawless no-man's-land, at the mercy of whatever summary justice the warped minds of the border guards might mete out.

I looked around; a lorry was being unpacked over to one side. The driver looked worried. A queue of nomadic types with overloaded donkeys were waiting at a smaller gate that opened onto the Iranian side of the border. A guard was waving people this way and that. I was filtered through a doorway at the side of the square courtyard. I showed my passport to a bored looking official. He barely glanced at it and waved me on. On the other side there were a few uniformed men talking amongst themselves resting their forearms on their machine guns, all but ignoring those coming through. Slightly relieved at the nonchalant attitudes that the border officials had displayed, I strode out amongst the baked and caked lorries parked on the other side.

I was now in Iran.

Once again it was dusk, and there was dust, and there was twilight. The colour of the air reminded me of sewage-stained water, as heat, tiredness and depression dragged me down both physically and mentally. I slumped under a lorry that was parked up for the night, only slightly worried that the driver might not check beneath it before setting off in the morning. I did not sleep well that night. The memory of the wolf the previous night troubled me continually. I did not know this at the time, but it was unlikely that a wolf would have approached such a mass of unnatural looking artefacts stinking of man. But I was exposed and vulnerable, and I felt this acutely. I needed a secure hole to hide in, to regather my disintegrating thoughts.

It was difficult to tell if it was actually morning in the red light. Lorries were revving and testing their headlights, creating an unwelcome glare for anyone like myself who had just woken up. I leaned up and held my hand, fingers aspray, in front of my face to shield my eyes. After accepting that the noise was not going to go away and leave me to fall back into my troubled dreams, I reluctantly and sullenly crawled out from under the lorry,

I had acquired a rucksack again, it contained my now obsolete sleeping bag. In the temperatures I was currently experiencing the sleeping bag and rucksack were for security, and to use as a pillow, more than anything else. The rucksack was literally something to do with my hands, to help stave off that naked feeling that claws at you when you have nothing. People cannot be trusted to not take advantage of each other's vulnerabilities. We need our shields, however symbolic they might be.

I lumbered along, waking up as I walked. On this side of the border the roads were a little more advanced, but not by much. Compressed earth and stones were replaced by more permanent looking materials.

I stuck my thumb out as I walked. Even the locals would have understood what this meant, as they had seen many Western hippies pass through the area. I knew they had a contempt for us. Some of this would have been due to their hyper-moral values colliding with our hyper-immoral values. But some of it must have been bafflement and anger at our having given up wealth and opportunity to share in their poverty. How stupid we must have seemed to them, throwing away and despising the very things they could only dream of and long for. But it seemed very spiritual to us to be poor, just as to them wealth seemed to be a kind of Holy Grail that would heal all their ills and give lifelong happiness. To us their attitude seemed to be a silly, cheap and disgustingly naïve way of looking at life. But until now we had never experienced real poverty, and conversely they had never experienced the disillusionment and even boredom that can come with abundant riches.

I did not have to wait long. To my surprise the two Iranian drivers from the previous day pulled up. The one who had given me a lift before beckoned for me to get in again. I climbed into his fast, slightly low slung car. We were off again at speed, but on more reliable roads than the ones we had endured in Turkey.

We were heading for Tehran, the capital of Iran, and this involved passing through long stretches of dry hilly scrubland and semi-desert. These areas were not inhabited by any settled communities, and it was easy to see why when you glanced down at the dry river beds and harsh, scorched gorges.

Much of the year nothing grew there, and the scampering of lizards would make you envious of the coolness they found in the agony of the cracked rock faces. The occasional lone locust turned on a stone and then catapulted itself blindly to a new location. A scratching, rasping sound filled the air, reminiscent of sand parched throats warning juicier creatures that they didn't really belong here, and would they be kind enough to lie down and die to make a feast for thousands of tiny mouths eyeing them up from under their stones.

We plummeted on at speed whenever the road straightened enough for fast driving, and we took corners, leaning with the centrifugal forces, hoping we would not meet the stubborn backside of a donkey parked in the middle of the road as we came round. The risk of skidding in sand was the biggest danger as we drove; much of the road was slick with dust. The finer grains had been gently, delicately deposited by drifting veils of wind. It was reminiscent of the rippling silk that might have passed this way during a more opulent age. Spewing dust as we went, we churned on for several hours. During this time the driver produced a bottle of whiskey. This was strange, as he was probably a Muslim by birth. He gave it to me, and even though I have never had a strong need for alcohol I accepted it gratefully, very gratefully, and proceeded to consume it.

My window was open and I tried to cool myself with the hot desert air, swinging one arm out while the other grasped the bottle. We tried to converse a bit, but his English was not good enough, and my mental coordination was becoming gradually compromised as I sipped at the burning liquid gold. Somehow in our pointless attempts to communicate we got onto the subject of the British Embassy in Tehran. This was mixed together with talk about my parents. It's anyone's guess what he understood by our conversation, but I now believe that his misunderstandings might have been my salvation in what was to come.

In the mirrors we often caught sight of the second car containing the driver's friend, off in the distance. For me, sitting in a fast car, drinking whiskey while it was snarling along through the dusty wilderness at speed, was a really cool thing to be doing. The car's engine must have been getting very hot, considering the amount of time we had been driving along in the volcanic stare of the sun. When the driver pulled up at a flat area next to the road I paid no heed. We were back in a hilly area again, with parched stream beds and bushes that could have doubled as skeletal claws. We had seen almost no traffic for several hours.

There was a quiet pause after we had halted, and I was aware that the driver was not looking at me or making any attempt to communicate. His companion pulled up in the other car about a hundred yards behind. He didn't get out. Eventually my driver leaned towards me and started to caress my thigh. I was heterosexual to the hilt, and even when very drunk the idea of sexual intimacy with another man made me feel a little sick. I removed his hand politely, as I normally did in such situations, shaking my head to underline my unwillingness to comply. At the time, because of my drunkenness, I don't think I was fully aware of the danger I was in. We were literally in the middle of nowhere. If he and his companion in the trailing car had wanted to get violent I would have been at a serious disadvantage. If they had injured me and thrown me into a ditch my body might not have been found for decades, or maybe not at all, had the local scavengers disassembled my bones to feed their young.

As usually happened in such circumstances, he made a few more attempts at getting his way and then gave up. After about five minutes of awkwardness, which largely washed over me in my inebriated state, I noticed his companion getting out of his car and walking towards us. He came over and talked to his friend in Iranian through the driver window, leaning down and looking at me as he did so. Eventually they seemed to come to a conclusion and nodded agreement to each other. Then his friend went back to his car. Without speaking, my driver started the engine and we were off again.

As you moved south through Europe, the standard sit-on toilet, with its nice private lockable space, toilet paper, and satisfying, cleansing flush, suddenly became something quite gross. You found yourself squatting on something resembling a shower tray with a hole in the middle, trying not to slip on the remains of someone else's explosive evacuation, while attempting to control your own stomach from over-enthusiastic release at both ends. If there was toilet paper available, it had a habit of blocking the hole in the middle of the squatting tray, and the only concession to a flush would be a jug of water at the side of the cubicle. It was pretty standard back then even for a holiday in Spain to be spoiled by a stomach bug. In fact it was almost expected that you would catch some form of diarrhoea if you went to one of the hotter European destinations.

The further East you went the worse this became, and toilets of any description were scarce. You soon found yourself squatting behind a rock giving the local flora and fauna a much needed moisture boost. Diarrhoea, which I suffered from for at least half my time out East, has a habit of draining a person of nutrition as well as of fluids. Food that goes in at one end can come out undigested at the other end. Much of the malnutrition and death occurring in Asia is caused not by a lack of available food, but by stomach diseases that disrupt the digestive process.

After several toilet stops, during which, to their credit, my two Iranian hosts didn't abandon me, we arrived in Tehran.

Chapter 15

The City of Glass

Tehran seemed to me to be a city of glass, as the hot sun reflected blindingly from the high-rise and mid-rise buildings. They were obviously chasing modernity in the same way as Turkey, but as I have already said, with a bit more success. Most of the roads in the city were either avenues, or very wide, making it impossible to cross them safely. Certainly pedestrians had been sidelined during the design phase of this part of the infrastructure. It looked as if Iran was mimicking America in this respect. Crossing the road was a form of Russian roulette, and required speed, agility and timing. I don't know how old people managed it. Even a young person needed to be somewhat of a gymnast to get to the other side of the road alive. It was as if the drivers could not see you, or dare not stop for fear of causing a pile up. Shortly after arriving I was walking along such an avenue. On the strip of centre island that ran the length of the road, two dogs had become trapped by the traffic. They lay facing each other, front paws outstretched, heads erect, an expression of resignation on their faces as they looked side on at the cars, exposing eye white in their anxiety. Clearly the two dogs were friends, or had become friends because of their mutual dilemma. They worried together rather than alone, but neither dog had come up with a solution. When they saw me on the other side, one of the dogs got up and ran into the road. It was instantly bowled over underneath a car. I remember seeing it rolling like a sausage as it passed under the car. The car didn't stop, or even slow. It died instantly. The other dog had got up to follow, now it just looked on, its jowls aghast. Then in sad resignation it laid down again, staring into the distance. For me this was a warning shot when it came to road safety in Tehran. I had no delusions that in the minds of some of the locals there wasn't much difference between hippies and stray dogs.

Giant pictures of the Shah of Iran occasionally appeared on the sides of buildings. To his enemies these over-inflations must have appeared ominous and threatening, They gave the impression that he was everywhere, and that he was watching. However to me they also hinted at desperation, at scrambling to cling to power. The less intelligent of his supporters might have been reassured by these gaseous ego balloons, but the thinkers amongst them will have realised that there was a large and aggressive Islamic fundamentalism spreading out from its fortification in the older generation, and in Iran's history. At the time I was completely ignorant of the nature of these forces even though I could sense a schizophrenia in this society. It was a case of modernity versus traditional values. These two principles were such polar opposites that violence was inevitable. But the brew was not yet hot enough. It was several years before the Shah had to flee to the West and the Muslim fundamentalists took over.

Once again the haunting need for a destination took me to a park bench. I sat there with my rucksack beside me, like so many tramps on so many park benches before me. Whatever anyone had said, the idea of rootless travel no longer seemed romantic to me. It was hard and lonely, and I felt I had squeezed every last drop out of the carefree, roving, vagabond gypsy myth.

It was very hot, and the sun glared in my eyes. Keeping clean had become a problem now. The temperature caused me to sweat profusely, even when at rest. Any grime clung to my body causing me to itch and scratch. Finding places to shower had become gradually harder from Athens onward. At about the same rate so had finding a reasonable toilet. Most hotels and hostels did have showers, and the locals all had their own facilities. But I was on the road most of the time, and so I had less access to these amenities now.

As I sat there, a chubby cheerful chap, obviously aware of the comedy of his own build, approached me smiling gleefully in a way that I had come to recognise.

"American?" he asked.

"No, English," I replied inaccurately, but answering the question he was really asking, which was, "Where are you from?"

"I am Ahmed," he offered.

"Stuart," I replied.

"Stee-uuu-warrt," he responded, his mouth twisting unnaturally and showing his teeth as he chewed my name. It seemed to be a form of tongue torture to him. He did eventually manage a reasonable rendering of the sound. He obviously had a sense of humour because he laughed at his own stumbling attempts. He sat next to me in a way that would have made me feel uncomfortable if it hadn't been for his genial, outgoing character. It seemed like the natural thing for such a friendly fellow to do. I was glad of the company but I had no delusions about what was coming next. Before long I was being led around, as if on a halter and with rosettes dangling from my horns. I was introduced to all his Iranian friends, who were both amused and curious in equal measure at this stranger from the West. This was of course in the days before the internet provided everybody with images and chatter from anywhere in the world. To them I was alien and exotic, and being young they wanted to explore my mind to help them form ideas of their own. Though I was unaware of it, this was not an entirely safe thing for them to be doing, with the rise of an intolerant regime gradually gathering strength in the background of Iranian politics. The ideas that I was presenting them with represented the worst excesses of our society, so I was probably unconsciously adding fuel to the fire, and giving credence to arguments of the opposition.

As well as introducing me to his friends, Ahmed made the mistake of introducing me to his parents. They were hospitable enough and allowed me to clean myself up and join them for meals. Their culture was of course new to me, so I don't know how many social gaffes I must have made while I was with them. I am clumsy enough in my own culture. They nevertheless allowed me to stay for a couple of days, after which I sensed that they had had enough of me.

Whether this was a hint or an altruistic gesture I do not know, but Ahmed had got the money together for me to travel by bus all the way to the Afghan border.

Chapter 16

Into the Dust Bowl

The bus journey was long, boring and hot. It lasted about 15 hours and I dozed a lot as the dusty scenery went by. Nothing significant or interesting happened on this part of the journey. I received no curiosity or attention from the people on the bus. Even though my skin was suntanned by now, I must still have been distinguishable as a Westerner because of my long hair and my rucksack. However I was all but ignored by my fellow passengers. I was glad when the journey was over.

The bus pulled up in a town called Taybad near the Afghan border.

The daylight was waning, and I started to dip in and out of alleys and dark side roads in the hope of finding somewhere that felt safe enough to bed down for the night. I found a wall down a small side street that I could sleep against and, hugging my sleeping bag for security, I dozed off again. The air filtered a coffee coloured light that might have been the remnant of a sandstorm. It slowly grew darker and darker until I was hidden.

In the morning I once again went round scrounging money for my wake up drink of tea, and for a bite of food. It was difficult to find a good target to beg from. I avoided locals and Iranians, no matter how wealthy they looked. Their reactions were likely to be hostile and unpredictable. Even if they did give me something it would either be with utter contempt, or with a pride in their own condescending generosity, lips pursed and delicately lowering notes nipped between thumb and forefinger, as if not wanting to touch the recipient. The few Westerners I did approach looked as poor as myself. That was until I spotted a couple of Americans who looked clean, and as if they had got off a plane fairly recently. These were not real travellers, they were just tourists despite their youth. What they were doing in this dust bowl of a town was anyone's guess. I had chosen correctly; they gave me enough money to buy a drink, and some breakfast at a local tea shop. I can't say they looked happy to be giving me money, but they were certainly wealthy enough to take a small hit like this.

It soon tumbled round to evening again. I had heard that it was necessary to have money to get into Afghanistan, something about a visa. I had also heard that it was possible to sell your own blood to a blood bank to earn enough money to travel further. Being squeamish about needles I didn't like the idea of this, but I could see little choice if I wanted to continue my journey.

The sky began to dull again, becoming lurid red and then black. It was time to find somewhere to bed down. As I started to search around for a likely spot to sleep, my attention was caught by some sounds from nearby. Mostly out of curiosity, I was drawn to the rich warble of a flute and the banging of drums further down the road. The sound was coming from a lorry park. I nosed my way cautiously into the unlit area at the back of a block of shops. I could just make out two lines of what looked like local vehicles. One had a flatbed trailer attached to it and I could just see little orange glows that brightened, then dimmed, then brightened again, and so on. The wobbly warbling of some windy reed instrument came from somewhere on the back of that dark trailer. So did the sound of drumming and the clanking of metal, as someone improvised with a petrol can. There was a strong smell of marijuana, and even in the dark I caught sight of billowing clouds of spent smoke.

I moved slowly until I was able to see over the edge of the trailer. There was a mixture of both hippies and Asian men. Some of latter wore the sort of baggy trousers that one normally associates with Aladdin pantomimes, and similarly they also wore loose turbans around their heads. However these were no pantomime characters. Their clothes were grubby and colourless, and their unwashed faces told me their jobs involved a certain amount of grease and oil. They were probably the drivers of the parked vehicles and their mates. I climbed up onto the trailer. I was barely noticed as I sat down near the edge of the group, listening to the beat and the rhythm going in and out of harmony, like dancers pulling away and then embracing, and then pulling away again. The squall of a more traditional instrument, played by one of the drivers, took over for a few minutes, and I imagined snakes dancing around only just out of range of my vision, away in the darkness, and sandy camels plodding splay-foot across impossible deserts, yet thriving like pompous kings surrounded by their treasure. There must have been at least ten people on the back of the trailer, and not everybody got a pull on the joint. I didn't mind. I was tired, so I just curled up and slept as best I could.

I awoke not really having slept much. Again I had spent most of the night in that twilight range, somewhere between sleep and wakefulness. The music had eventually stopped in the early hours, and now the scene was somewhat reminiscent of 'the morning after'. However here there were no empty bottles, and no smell of vomit, just people lying around curled up, some without blankets. The group was mostly made up of men, but I noticed a couple of girls amongst hippies, who were curled up next to their partners.

In this region a Western woman travelling on her own could be considered insane, without too much question. It was dangerous enough for a Western woman to travel in company, especially if she was insensitive to the local religious customs. Some of these girls and their partners may have been using local transport rather than hitch-hiking. The latter of these two options being almost as dangerous as going it alone, the former being the much more sensible choice.

This part of the world, and especially the next part of the journey eastwards, was a predator's paradise. It had long stretches of road that were completely uninhabited, where gangs could lie in wait, rape, kill and steal with impunity, and drag the bodies over a hill out of sight. The sparse population in these regions was what made it unlikely that bodies would ever be found, even if by some miracle the bodies had survived dismemberment by wild animals.

I had heard stories of bandits in that area. One tale in particular was of a vanload of Westerners who had been ambushed and robbed resulting in several of their number being killed. Personally, I would say they were lucky, inasmuch as some of them had escaped to tell the tale.

I climbed off the trailer and made my way out onto the street. My priority for the day was to find the blood bank and get myself a bit of cash. As I have said, I didn't like the idea but at the time I felt I had no other options. I spent several hours that morning trying to locate the blood bank, with eventual success. I was surprised when I went in to find a fairly well-appointed clinic that looked hygienic and safe. There was an Iranian female nurse who could speak English, and who was reassuringly prim and tidy. She seemed to be the only member of staff, and her only roles appeared to be taking blood and administering vaccinations. She filled in a few forms for me, after asking my date of birth and then checking my passport. I was tense, never having given blood before, and I had little idea what to expect. She told me to lie down on the bed, and after cleaning the spot, she forced the large calibre needle into my arm. It didn't hurt much but I tried not to look at it, or think about what was happening as I laid there. It was hot and I was sweating a lot already, but the stress from having my arm punctured, and the thought of my blood leaking into a transparent plastic bag, made me sweat even more. Eventually my stomach felt as if it was being wrung out like a wet dishcloth, and my forehead started to feel cold despite the heat. I was starting to see spots in front of my eyes. The nurse, who was obviously a professional, could see that I was in trouble, so she halted the procedure. I felt embarrassed, especially in front of a woman, because I had nearly fainted. I had however managed to give half the quantity required, and so I got half the payment for the blood. The payment was given in American dollars, a popular currency in Asia in those days because it tended to hold its value, unlike the fickle local monies.

Chapter 17

The Land of the Reluctant Wolf

Wolves are not like dogs even though genetically they are clearly the same species. Maybe one could say the same about the Afghan people. There is still a wildness in them that won't be tamed to civilisation. We admire this of course, even though we also fear it. It is strength, but it is also weakness. Their tribes fight each other because without war, the lives of the menfolk would be meaningless. Sadly, their pride is all they have. This is a land of warrior horsemen, many of whom carry rifles. I would not have found it surprising if they played polo with the heads of their enemies. There are no laws here, you are at the mercy of the strong, and mercy is in short supply in this place. Any laws that do exist are scantily clad and feeble, especially against the brutal strength of the tribe.

The border crossing point was not very substantial, and I did not have a great deal of confidence in the hospitality of the border guards should I start to suffer from dehydration. If I had dried out to a dust caked stick I doubt they would have as much as glanced in my direction. After about an hour of worry, to my surprise and relief a bus appeared like a mirage in the distance, shimmering and rippling at first, and then resolving itself into something less magical as it rattled towards me. This border post actually had a bus service. I could not believe it!

I climbed aboard and, like so many rude bus drivers the world over, this one did not acknowledge me, but just stared ahead with eyes front. I showed the driver a few Afghan coins I had picked up while in Iran. He nodded. I dropped them in his bag. Then he engaged the gears, there was a loud grating noise as he did so. He reversed his crippled bus around before making it hobble off down the road towards the town of Herat.

The bus danced from left to right like a demented party goer about to throw off all his clothes. The clanking and clattering that I was hearing just had to be bits dropping off as the Sellotape and string gave way.

Apart from the smell, I had not noticed the nature of my travelling companions. At the back of the bus, like naughty school children, was a tightly huddled flock of sheep. In the middle of the crush, a shepherd sat nonchalantly dozing in the miasma.

I squeezed myself onto one of the densely packed seats and hugged my rucksack on my knees.

There were also a few women on the bus wearing blue burkas. Like most Westerners I found these sinister. They seemed like a kind of portable dungeon, as the women looked out from the grated window at the world outside. The burkas also looked heavy and hot, especially in this climate. The men in this society must have been afraid of the dangers of their own sexuality. Ironically burkas probably had their root in a desire to protect women and society from this powerful force. We in the West are doing nothing to encourage these people away from such draconian methods with our examples of promiscuity and familial disintegration.

Eventually we arrived at Herat. I never travel well unless I am in the front seat of a vehicle, and have had a meal to ballast my stomach. My empty stomach felt as if it had been kicked around like a football. I felt perfectly sick, the effect being compounded by the stink, the wobble and the heat, as well as the cramped conditions and the hard bottom-smashing seats. I alighted from the bus slowly, taking the steps one at a time rather than leaping down in an exuberant, energetic young person way.

Outside, there was a crowd at the steps of the bus. Some were jostling to get on, others were trying to get the attention of people getting off. One man waved his hand in my face and shouted "cheap hotel mister, cheap hotel". I ignored him, not out of rudeness, but I was just too weary for any kind of interaction with anyone.

I realised, as I recovered from my nausea, that this would not be a good town for sleeping rough. This was a land in which you were extremely vulnerable unless you had family connections of some sort.

Once again I had the problem of being penniless. I worried about this, since I didn't fancy begging in this relatively threatening environment. Even my fellow Westerners appeared to be cut from a rougher cloth than normal.

Then I clamped onto an idea. What if I were to offer my services as a tourist hassler, like the men at the bus stop? Westerners often ignored locals who were trying to solicit their custom for the various hotels. But if a fellow Westerner were to approach them quietly and recommend accommodation they would be more likely to listen.

Before I go any further with my story I need to redefine the word 'hotel'. The English dictionary defines a hotel as 'an establishment providing accommodation and meals for travellers and tourists'. This is fair enough, and I suppose this definition does actually include Afghan hotels as well. However the Western mind usually has all sorts of additional clutter hanging on the definition of the word 'hotel'. For example most Westerners expect a hotel to provide a comfortable bed with an adequate mattress and bedding, a bedside lamp, a lockable door, easy access to a decent shower and toilet, possibly *en suite* tea making facilities and television, and some sort of dining facilities.

However in Afghanistan nothing more than a cubicle containing a wooden bed frame with a string net base passed as hotel accommodation. This varied a lot of course depending on how much you could pay, but such scant accommodation was quite normal, both in Afghanistan and the rest of Asia.

I walked up and down the street briefly checking out a few places that presented themselves as hostels or hotels. Eventually I opted for one that I could tout convincingly, without having the comeback that is the inevitable consequence of lying. It was reasonably clean and had a communal area in which people sat on a carpeted floor to eat, drink tea and smoke marijuana. I managed to communicate my idea to the owner. Finally, he nodded in that strange way that some Eastern people nod, more like a mixture of nodding and shaking, and with a flourish of his hand, through this body language alone he suggested that I give it a try. My deal was, that he give me somewhere to stay, and food to eat, and perhaps some marijuana, and I would find him customers.

This worked fairly well, so for a few days I actually had employment. But I soon grew restless again. I also had problems jelling with the Afghans running the place and my fellow hippies. When they smoked marijuana together I felt left out, and tended to lounge on the sidelines of the carpet rather than sitting in amongst the group. How much of this was my personal tendency to feel alienated in groups, and how much of it was real, I do not know. The marijuana, with its psychological magnifying effect, wasn't helping at all. It was aggravating my negative state of mind yet further.

Eventually I left Herat and headed for Kabul. I hitch-hiked this part of the journey, even though the road I was travelling had as bad a reputation as any when it came to bandits and abusers.

However the wilderness that I had to travel through did not close its teeth on me. And to be fair to that wilderness, those who attack travellers are not truly part of it. I made it to Kabul.

This time I did not seek work, instead I targeted Westerners with my begging skills. I stayed in primitive accommodation. This was nothing but an empty ground floor room that would probably have passed as a brick shed or an outhouse in the West. It had no windows but it did have a small vent hole at the top of one of the walls. This was literally no more than a square hole, it had no grate or grille in it.

The only furnishing was one of those almost ubiquitous wooden framed, string net beds. I lay sprawled on it in the heat, listening to the lazy, laid-back tongues of Americans in conversation at the nearby rooftop café, and watching the lizards miraculously traverse the walls and ceiling of my claustrophobic cell. I wanted privacy, but it was too hot to close my door for long. When I opened the door I could see a sheet of material tied at the corners, sagging listlessly on the rooftop above. It provided the customers with some relief from the scorching sun, but there was no real escape. Even the young like myself had their energy and their fluids sucked from them by that gigantic all-consuming vampire in the sky. Many were left as slouching, pot bellied, semi-demented husks, struggling to keep their eyes open, passing chillums of marijuana from person to person.

The little glasses of hot sweet tea next to them may well have been their only protection, the unnoticed, unsung defender that kept them from getting too dehydrated.

I was starting to feel despondent again, but I decided that I hadn't come all that way just to spread myself limply across an uncomfortable bed frame. So even though diarrhoea was sapping my strength, and that glorious globe of burning gold was bearing down disapprovingly on all beneath it, I still decided that I really needed to explore Kabul. I dragged myself up from the bed into a standing position, and then plodded out to the street to join the mad dogs and Englishmen in the noonday sun.

I tried to stay in the shade as I walked the length of the street.

Afghan shops were usually open fronted, and most resembled market stalls. There were the usual commodities like fruit and vegetables as well as hanging legs of meat that were often festooned with flies. Most of the produce on sale was in the form of raw material rather than pre-cooked, pre-packaged or pre-worked. As well as fruit, veg and meat, there was also cloth and grain. Clothes, blankets, carpets and ornaments made up a large percentage of the ready worked goods. The shopkeepers wisely hung back in the black shadows and moved as little as possible, making them almost invisible when viewed from the bright glare of the street. They sat squatting or cross legged on rude carpets, their faces like burnt chestnuts, a motley brown that lent itself to old age and character.

Kabul was a city with roads and cars, electricity and infrastructure. But it had a shabby look to it that was common in third world cities. It looked as if it was making a badly financed or token attempt at modernisation. One felt that those in authority were perhaps too wrapped up in inner politics or military conflict to be bothered about the wellbeing of their people.

I also noticed that the city had a more unusual air to it. It gave me the feeling that I was on the edge of the wild. This was a borderland between two domains, where the fierce hills and mountains nearby spilled over into the city, and where the city intruded on the untamed lands beyond it. If this was an attempt by some Afghans to isolate themselves from their history and to move on, then it wasn't really working.

Once again I was drawn to a park I had noticed just across the road. The slightest suggestion of shade and a place to sit quietly was enough. Once again the simple basic need for a destination was working almost obsessively on my mind. Once again I was suffering from park bench syndrome, the need for nothing more than a place to be.

I didn't find a park bench, and I soon realised that to refer to this area as a park was a bit of an overstatement. It was just a piece of ground with a few immature trees on it, that hadn't been built on yet. There was a path worn into the ground winding between the trees, and a few Afghans standing at intervals who appeared to be selling stuff.

As I walked, movement at the foot of one of these salesmen caught my eye. A grey animal about eighteen inches in length was straining painfully at a leash of rope. Its companion, an almost identical animal, was equally distressed. Though they resembled puppies, they had no appealing eyes for man. They stared keenly into the distance as they tried to get away from the object of their terror. The man stood over them, ominously tall and slim; he was completely dispassionate to their plight.

I caught a slight sneer on his small mouth as I approached, and I could see his shadowy but intelligent eyes checking me out as I walked towards him.

He was a hunter, at ease with the practical side to death and suffering when it was pitted against his own personal survival or profit.

I was fascinated by these creatures from the empty places beyond the city. Maybe their mother had been bothering sheep, or maybe it was just that her fur was worth selling. Whatever the reason, these wolf cubs were now orphans. And they were experiencing fear that they could never have imagined in their cosy den somewhere high up in the echoing crags. They were longing for the soft snout of their mother and the reassuring massage of her tongue. Ironically they wanted to resemble puppies again, more than anything else in the world.

I had always found animals fascinating. From the age of ten I had kept lots of different exotic pets.

I had had an iguana, an alligator, geckos, common lizards, grass snakes, giant millipedes, stick insects, chipmunks, terrapins, tortoises, fish and birds. I often took these to school to get attention. I was not a naturally popular child so this gave me a short burst of celebrity with the other children. However I do not think this celebrity carried over to the female teachers.

There was no legislation governing the import, capture or care of such creatures when I was a child, and few of these animals were captive bred back in those days. Most had been taken straight from their wild environments, and had often been transported in inadequate containers to countries with climates that were nothing like the climates they had been born into. On arrival, they were thrust into a situation in which there were lots of diseases to which they had no immunity.

The people who bought them had no idea how to look after them, because as yet no database of experience had been built up, and so no specialist books existed. The mortality rate among such pets was very high.

I had of course never had a wolf. A wolf, most people would agree, is the epitome of coolness. It is intelligent, affectionate, courageous and fierce. What man, whether warrior or hippie, doesn't want to identify with a wolf? What woman, no matter how demure, isn't attracted to the idea of a wolf-like man? To be able to befriend and control such an animal would make me into a king in the land of the cool. So I did the only sensible thing that I could, I swapped my sleeping bag for it.

I had had a fair bit of experience dealing with canine kind.

When I was a child we had had an Alsatian bitch called Bonnie. She was very protective of me and often escorted me around the village in which we then lived. One day some workmen were digging a hole at the front of the hotel, of which my father was the landlord. For a five-year-old child, such a novelty was completely irresistible. But my incessant chattering and questioning got on the nerves of one of the workmen. He reached out to give me some money for sweets, so as to get rid of me, and the dog, misunderstanding the gesture, bit him. Luckily my father was able to calm him down with a few free pints. Bonnie was killed two years later in Carlisle, when she was hit by a lorry outside our new home.

A few years after that we acquired our next dog, Charlie. Charlie, a Boxer-Labrador, was a bouncing bundle of uncontrollable energy. He was also fundamentally a vicious dog, and he needed to be. My mother had acquired him from a police inspector who was a friend of the family. She had recently been widowed, and she wanted a dog like Charlie to protect the licensed premises on which we lived. The problem was he also had to double as a family dog.

I was tasked with the job of walking him. He was a young dog of about nine months old, and he had never learned to walk at heel. So he constantly pulled at the leash, making exercising him quite an unpleasant experience. Even a choke chain did not seem to make much difference. Whenever he saw another dog across the road he would go into a frenzy, and I would have a serious struggle holding onto him. When I took him to a park and let him off the lead, he would immediately plunge into fights with every other male dog that he came across. However he was extremely polite and submissive to the wishes of any bitches he came across.

Many dogs strolled the streets unaccompanied in those days. Sometimes Charlie would disappear for an hour or two while I was walking him. This was very distressing for me. I would comb the river bank and nearby playing fields for him. Then long after I had given up hope, he would reappear. Over the years that followed the area nearby developed a problem with vicious dogs.

I went back to the hotel, pleased with my purchase and dreaming of the future we would have together, man and wolf in perfect harmony. Memories of the book *Call of the Wild* were still strong in my mind, having read it three years earlier in school. Though I had often fantasised about it, I had never truly believed I would ever live out such a story in real life.

When I got back to the hotel I went to the rooftop café and lounged around with the other hippies, who were from various nations around the world. My wolf on his leash of rope caught the interest of most of them.

Everyone was mentally addled by the rippling heat of the sun and the vast quantities of marijuana they had consumed. In Afghanistan the pieces of marijuana they regarded as crumbs could have easily been sold as quid deals back home in the UK.

There was a German girl sitting at a nearby table with some companions. She made the effort to come slowly, unsteadily, over to where I was. She seemed to be showing a strong maternal interest in my wolf cub. At the time the cub was trying to hide behind plant pots, no doubt looking for a den to get itself out of the blistering heat and dazzling light.

Even though I was as mentally bombed out as everybody else, that niggling nuisance common sense was starting to bothering me. And eventually it managed to prise its way into my brain.

I realised I would have a lot of problems getting my wolf across borders. And I figured that finding sheep to feed it on might be a bit difficult, that is, without getting into trouble with local farmers. I also had an inkling that training it would make the discipline problems I had had with Charlie look extremely trivial. In short, I realised that my journey would be made a lot easier if I didn't have my loyal companion White Fang tagging along with me.

Since the German girl was cooing and crooning over him, the solution was simple. I would give him to her. She accepted him gratefully, no doubt feeling honoured that fate or karma or whatever had brought them together. Who knows, maybe she made a brilliant surrogate wolf-mum, and maybe she accrued eye watering quantities of cool points in the process? After that I never saw the wolf again, nor for that matter did I ever see the German girl again.

At this point I was emotionally depleted, exhausted and depressed. And I was seriously considering turning back and going home. However I stubbornly decided to continue my journey eastwards.

From Kabul the Hippie Trail continues through Jalalabad and then on to the Khyber Pass border post. The Khyber Pass was one of those regions with an almost legendary reputation for violence. On the other side of the border inside Pakistan, men strolled around with rifles in a way that was very reminiscent of the wild west. The standing advice was to get through that area as quickly as possible, and whatever you do, don't try to stare anyone down.

By now I was broke again, so when I got to the border I could not pay the border guards the random fee they were charging people to get across. So I spent the day sitting on what used to be a railway platform back in the time when the British Empire tried desperately to control things here. In those days trains had frequently travelled through the pass bringing troops and weapons to this unruly area.

This border post was a busy one. But unlike the one at the Turkey-Iran border, this border post only had small local lorries queuing to get through.

They were colourful affairs, festooned with ornaments and painted flowers. They were quirky to say the least, and looked a bit like gypsy wagons. The drivers were clearly a fun loving lot who obviously wanted to bring a smile to other people's faces. They contrasted with the humourless men who had dangerous looking black beards and whose eyes and clothing seemed to be smeared with gunpowder, giving them a volatile look.

In the late afternoon I noticed a mass movement of people towards the border, and so I joined the flow. Nobody challenged me or asked for my passport this time, I just walked across the border with a bunch of other people. I still have no real explanation for this, except that I must have been mistaken for a member of some large group that was allowed across.

Once on the other side, I could see that the rumours of danger and violence had to be true. The number of rifles I counted while casting my eyes cautiously around was unnerving. I was in what appeared to be a one horse town, in which smiles were a rare commodity, and were probably frowned upon darkly should somebody dare to even curl a lip in humour. Liquor was almost certainly illegal here, and one can only thank God for that. If I had had to choose a name for this town then 'Tomb Stone' would most certainly have been on my list.

I didn't want to hang around in Tomb Stone, so I once again decided to go with the flow. I noticed people climbing onto one of the painted lorries. Its canopy had been removed. This meant it was now a high sided, open backed lorry. I nonchalantly joined the crowd and climbed aboard. I didn't have a sleeping bag or a rucksack with me at this stage, so maybe this and my full-on suntan helped me not to be identified as a Westerner, and so I blended in with the general crowd.

The lorry clawed its way up the meandering mountain road, jostling its occupants and snarling every now and again as the driver changed gear. It was headed for Peshwar about 50 kilometres away, and doggedly continued on its struggle along this less than perfect road.

It paused on one occasion so that the occupants could watch an unfolding drama, as an overloaded donkey began to lose its footing on a scree slope. Its hind legs were slipping off the precarious path leading up the unstable surface. It was kicking out in panic, making its already tenuous situation far worse. One of the drivers managed to unload it so that the other could drag it back up onto the path. The lorry drove on.

Then it paused again. This time a man with a rifle was sneaking around in the bed of a stream below us. He disappeared amongst the rocks and the lorry moved on.

There was no more drama to watch so we continued on. When we got to Peshwar I disembarked when the lorry had to slow down at a busy crossroads. If there was a fare for this journey then I had managed to dodge it. There were no cries of outrage as I jumped off, so this must have been fairly normal behaviour.

A few days later I arrived in Lahore. I climbed out of a van into the crowded streets as it inched along through the throng. I was getting my first taste of the confusion and turmoil so prevalent in many of the overpopulated cities of Asia. While it was by no means the most populous city in this part of the world, it began to give me a flavour of what was to come.

Asia is an alien place to the Western mind, and as I looked up at some of the apparently random telephone and power cabling criss-crossing the street I felt disorientated. The three wheeled motorised rickshaw cabs were also new to me. They were strange. I watched them toddle along the roads threatened by much larger vehicles moving faster and with more momentum.

Bicycles weaved in and out of the halting tangle of traffic. Young men going to work on lite motorbikes leaned over and waited until a gap presented itself in the fuming congestion.

As I walked down side streets the crush got denser, but it became more pedestrian and less vehicular. Even so the odd van, or car, or lorry, sometimes pushed its way through the crowd at a snail's pace. The Pakistani burkas I noticed were more frequently black, and didn't have grilles hiding the eyes like the blue Afghan burkas. I don't know if this difference was significant to anybody, perhaps it was nothing more than a regional fashion.

I eventually found a cheap hotel that was full of Westerners. I have to reiterate here that the word 'hotel' does not adequately describe these cheap Eastern hotels to the Western mind. To us the word 'hotel' suggests a certain amount of luxury, not the threadbare accommodation that one frequently came across when travelling on a budget out East. In fact even homeless shelters in Britain were usually much more comfortable than Asian hotels.

The hotel had a quadrangle area in its centre, surrounded by three storeys of rooms with walkways around the upper levels. The quadrangle was the communal area and had a café. It was usually packed with travellers.

This particular hotel was one of those focal points for hippies and travellers to congregate, and to find a bit of relief from the bizarreness of it all through interaction with other Europeans and with Westerners in general. That relief could be tentative though given the amount of drug taking that was going on, and the fact that many of the Westerners themselves came from cultures that didn't sit totally comfortably with each other.

There were the French who were aloof and snooty, and mocked everybody else's style-less lack of taste while remaining oblivious to their own tragic superficiality.

There were the Germans at the other end of the scale, blunt, socially crude, taciturn and insecure about their recent history, the men often adopting deep monotone voices when they spoke, as if that were somehow cool.

The Americans were laid-back and full of themselves. Some would affect a Vietnam veteran posture in their combat jackets. Or maybe they weren't affecting it at all, maybe it was for real.

There were the self righteous Dutch, who were determined to prove that they were not German by pumping out all sorts of liberal indignation in what was clearly an embryonic form of today's political correctness.

There was the occasional Aussie, going in the wrong direction, missing his beer and opening his heart to the not unsympathetic German.

And of course there were the British, a motley crew who seemed to be a bit of everything and yet nothing in particular.

I sat amongst this cacophony of cultures feeling invisible. The truth is it was a dark place, and the stress and anxiety was apparent in everyone. This was not helped by the mood enhancing effects of the marijuana.

Some people's eyes stared into the distance, worried about where to go next, and becoming aware of the potential precariousness of their current situation. They were far from home and had suddenly realised that their normal safety nets were no longer there.

This was also a claustrophobic place. It was crowded outside in the street, and it was crowded inside in the quadrangle. I was not keen on it. The only positive thing I found there was the milk tea they served. The tea was made completely with milk and no water. This hot, sweet drink was very pleasant, and will have nourished many a depleted body *en route* further east.

I was already itching to move on, and the dream of a bright, cool, green place with wide open spaces had become an obsession. I was too far away by now to go back home, so the only way to go was forward, further east towards the Himalayas.

There were not many representatives of the local culture amongst the residents and customers in the quadrangle. It was unusual to see someone of Pakistani origin in the crowd. Most locals understandably were not willing to degrade themselves by joining us. However every now and again a sycophant would try to attach himself to Western culture by joining in with our inactivities. One sensed that such people had social issues with their own kind, and were somehow trying to compensate by chasing the modernity of Western culture. I do not include those I met in Turkey and Iran in this group, they seemed to be genuinely politically motivated, and possibly seeking some higher good for their communities.

In amongst the crowd I had noticed a young man of Pakistani origin who seemed to be trying too hard to ingratiate himself with the cool laid-back Westerners reclining around. He was stressed out and uptight, not something that hippies or their subtypes liked or had any patience with. Even if you were falling apart at the seams you were expected to cover it over. You could say that the hippies had a kind of 'stiff upper lip' philosophy of their very own. He was sitting a little back from the fringe of the group, and suddenly he began to cry. He didn't sob, but the copious tears streaming down his face gave him away immediately. No one reached out to comfort him; everyone was too absorbed in themselves, their marijuana, and their ego trips, to bother with a weakling like that.

If he thought he was going to get sympathy or comfort for his tears, then he didn't understand how hard and cruel the hippie scene really was. When you scratched off its colourful but superficial coating of 'love' and 'peace' there was nothing there but selfishness.

I set off for India, aiming north-east for the Himalayas.

Chapter 18

Higher and Higher

The higher I went the cooler it became. The increase in elevation was very gradual, hardly noticeable from hour to hour, but eventually I found myself in a land of coiling mists and enigmatic echoing cracks from somewhere high above. I was not in the highest Himalayas, which average at about 6,000 metres above sea level. I was 1,000 to 2,000 metres above sea level, but there was already a marked difference in the climate. Conifers grew randomly up the sides of the steep valleys, breaking rocks away from their parent mountains as they desperately and mercilessly sought nourishment with their muscular roots. Any settlements stayed in the valley bottoms, but remained above the torrential, hissing rivers that carved their way through the stone and rubble below. These small towns hugged the road, too insecure to clamber up the steep, forbidding slopes.

Such altitudes were for the wild animals. If people did go there, they tended to follow the undisciplined trails made by these animals rather than impose their own pathways. One felt that the people here feared the spirits of this place. For me there was always a mild sense of ominous threat coming from those untamed slopes. I stuck to the road, which was taking me slowly higher into the sky.

It was while hitch-hiking on this road that I caught up with a group of three other Westerners. All three were young men in their twenties, two were French and one was German. They were amiable enough and allowed me to travel with them. As in all groups there was that unconscious, and very intuitive, hierarchy at play. Joel, one of the French men, was clearly the leader, the others took their cues from him. I was the newcomer and the youngster in the group so I just followed the lead of the others, who from my point of view all seemed very together and mature. A small difference in age of a few years seems to make a massive difference when you are young.

As it turned out, these guys had smuggled some morphine across the India-Pakistan border with a view to selling it in Manali, in north India.

Four people was a bit too much of a crowd to get a lift, so we split up again and I travelled on my own. I was not in a good state of health at this point. As I have already mentioned, I was starting to become very depressed and generally fatigued. This will have been at least partly due to the draining effect of stomach bugs such as dysentery, but it was probably also due to my general state of health at the time.

Because finding somewhere to wash can be a problem when you are on the road, and because you sweat a lot in hot countries, you often end up tormented by itching. This happened to me more and more as I travelled across Asia. Gradually my legs, which seemed to itch more than the rest of my body, had become covered with small sores from insect bites and my from scratching.

At this point I was very vulnerable to infection. The fact that the climate in the mountains was cooler will have helped, but it was still warm, and far more humid than down below on the plains.

Further up the road, the ground above it opened out into layered paddy fields. These were higher than the cut of the river, so for the most part I could not see them. However I felt less enclosed and oppressed by the steep valley walls as they backed away from the river itself.

After walking for about an hour I got a lift from a local lorry. The lorry was adorned with all the fun loving paraphernalia that the drivers in this part of the world seem to favour. The driver himself was a cheerful, bestubbled, local man. He sparked with the kind of wild recklessness needed to negotiate some of the more dangerous mountain roads in this area. Recklessness, humour and maybe a bit of insanity seemed to blend together so that it was difficult to tell them apart.

This particular road was not in a bad a state of repair. It was wide enough for the lorry, and none of the drops at the side of the road were precipitous, though we would probably still have been killed if we had gone over the side into the river below.

The decorations on these lorries often involved religious symbols and pictures of various gods, all mixed in amongst painted flowers and other colourful patterns and shapes. The driver did not speak English, but his nutty brown face and cheerful disposition made him very pleasant company. I felt that the he loved his home and that he was somewhat proud of its magical character.

We got to Manali and he dropped me off at the fringe of the town. I was now at about 2,000 metres above sea level and it had become possible to detect some thinness of the air.

Looking to my left I saw a temple with fierce, fiery toothed wooden gargoyles that resembled bulldogs. They were painted in bright colours and sat at the top of totem pillars on either side of the temple entrance. I later discovered that this part of Manali was the Tibetan quarter. Many Tibetan Buddhists had fled religious and cultural persecution when the Chinese invaded Tibet in 1949. They had lived in north India ever since, alongside the local population who were mainly Hindus.

As I walked, it felt as if each breath I took was a little bit vacuous, as if I was breathing in a portion of empty space along with the air that I took in. I had to draw bigger breaths to get the satisfaction of having full lungs. Walking, especially when carrying a load, took more effort in these mountains. If I was ascending a slope I found that I had to stop more frequently to catch my breath.

To my right the river was about 50 metres away. Between the road and the river was an open space that was occupied by a handful of traders, including a Tibetan *chai* shop that also sold cooked food. Because it was so cheap, this ended up being somewhere that I regularly went to eat. Five rupees bought me a filling bowl of noodles in a watery meat soup of some sort. In those days five rupees was about 25 pence in English money.

Hygiene was not a concept that got a great deal of attention in this part of India. I suspect that apart from a bit of religious washing, there was nothing to hinder the plethora of different viruses and bacteria that thrived there.

There were flies as well, swarms of them. Many would land on the food after having feasted on human faeces down by the river. My delicate Western stomach had far less resistance to these bugs than most of the locals. I felt drained and sickly for most of the two months I spent in Manali.

As I walked up the road, the town became a bit denser and more substantial, with rickety two storey buildings instead of shacks. Even though we were many miles from the sea, these looked as if they had been knocked together out of driftwood planks and scavenged nails.

The roofs were constructed of randomly hewn, heavy stone slabs, which should, strictly speaking, have brought the whole building down under their weight. Some had corrugated iron sheets as roofing. The electrical or telephone wiring that did exist was such a chaotic tangle that only an autistic savant would have had any chance of maintaining or repairing it.

The town of Manali was quite small. Spreading to the left of me it only extended a short way up the valley. The few houses that did climb the side of the valley began their ascent at the Tibetan quarter following a small river gully. The buildings were mostly log structures with glassless windows, and balconies that looked out over the valley. Some kind of daub was used to fill in any draughty gaps that would otherwise occur with this kind of structure. They were built well clear of any seasonal torrents that tore down from the mountain tops their lacy curtains of spray and mist spiralling insanely and bouncing from rock to rock.

One such building was a *chai* shop, high up along the gully. This had areas for sitting and enjoying the view. It was only a very small place and its tables and chairs were made of the same rough sawn planks and poles that constituted many of the houses. Westerners, those who weren't too stoned to make the climb, seemed to favour this place. The air here was thin and ethereal, and so were the emotions of the stoned individuals sitting around smoking dope. Everything seemed to echo with emptiness here, even though the place itself was fresh, expansive and beautiful.

As I got further into the town I noticed a bridge to my right, going over the river. From this point the road went even higher into the Himalayas. I have often wondered what was up there, and in some respects I regret not having travelled further. But this was as high as I would go. After Manali, I would start rolling back downhill again.

There were plenty of Westerners here, and as usual most of these spoke at least some English. It was hard to tell in this place which travellers had money and which ones didn't. Everybody had become so laid-back in their dress and their mannerisms that it was difficult to distinguish between destitute hippies like myself and American tourists who were essentially doing an early form of what later became known as the 'gap year'.

Even thought we were in the mountains and it was considerably cooler than at lower altitudes, it was still warm enough to cause sweating. Most Westerners wore loose fitting flannel clothing made of some kind of lightweight cloth. As I have already mentioned, the trousers that some people wore resembled pyjamas. Loose fitting tops of similar material were also commonly worn. Many travellers adorned themselves with beads and religious symbols that sagged around their necks. The Buddhist Yin-Yang symbol was one of the pieces of jewellery that was sometimes worn by the hippies.

Some did that meandering walk that stoned individuals often do, as if time doesn't matter, and as if efficiency was somehow the arch enemy of all things good and wholesome. Western girls drifted from shop to shop, examining scarves, blissfully rubbing them against their cheeks, while inhaling the scent from an infinite variety of joss sticks before staring dreamily off into the distance. Their tripped-out boyfriends stood in disjointed postures gawping at passers-by, and being ignored by the locals who had seen it all before.

In those days some of the roads in Manali were roughly paved or muddy, and many of the shops were situated up narrow alleys that were accessed by crude stone slab steps. In these alleys one found more fly infested *chai* shops.

I lit up a *beedi* cigarette as I walked. A packet of these diminutive fags had been given to me by the lorry driver before I got out of the cab. It was a small, brown, crude looking thing, composed of tobacco flakes, wrapped in some other species of leaf. *Beedis* are closed up at the front end, and taper down towards the smoked end, resembling a tiny angel's bugle. These were common in India, and it was possible to buy them cheaply just about anywhere.

I asked around to find out if there was any accommodation available. I was now thinking in terms of somewhere rented instead of a hostel or a hotel. I badly needed the psychological shielding of a private space, a simple wall between me and everybody else in the world.

I was pointed towards a ridge high up on the valley side, where I was told that there was a building for rent. I chose a gradual meandering route that took me through some trees and past a temple that was dedicated to a 14th century woman called Hidimba, who is worshipped as a goddess. Why she is worshipped is very unclear, since all she seemed to do was to encourage other men to try to kill her brother. Someone did succeed in this task, and so she married him.

While this chap must have been quite fierce and manly and all that, he was obviously a little bit intellectually challenged. Most men would have had a bad feeling about this woman.

I arrived at the level area that had been pointed out to me, which was wide enough for a few fields to be cultivated on it. There were also one or two simple one storey buildings that had been constructed along the ridge path. I asked about accommodation as I went, and eventually came across a smartly built wooden structure. It had a balcony along most of the front of the building, with a glassed-in window extending the length of the balcony. There was only one room, the floor was packed earth, and it had a wood burning stove in its centre. A young Asian couple lived next door in the same building. Their home was no bigger than a pantry, perhaps that's what it was. But these two local people seemed content in their cramped conditions. To me they seemed to have an uncluttered life that was quite simply happy. Both were attractive and cheerful individuals. I do not honestly know if that is how they themselves truly felt, or if that was just my naïve, romantic, Western notion. It could have been that they were as jealous as hell of the wealth that I could so easily go back to in the West. Perhaps they would have given almost anything to swap places with me.

When I indicated that I hoped to move in next door they seemed quite happy with the idea. The girl disappeared off down the trail. It was not long before an older local man who had no English turned up and indicated that the rent would be five rupees (25 pence) a week. I realised that it would be very easy to find five rupees a week to pay the rent. By now my pseudo-spiritual left-wing extremism had become a little muted by the educational rigours of real life, and so I happily accepted this minuscule fee for the sake of a roof over my head.

I laid down on the dry earth floor, ignoring the view through the window across to the other side of the valley. I had no possessions, only the clothes I was wearing. The flies were once again buzzing around the weeping scabs that covered my legs. I was tired, depressed and lonely, but I was also far too anxious to sleep. While I was in no obvious physical danger, I knew that on some intangible level, and on some invisible plane, I was in jeopardy.

I now believe that during my short adult life my mind had become inextricably trapped in some sort of unstoppable spiritual machinery and only a miracle would be able to set me free.

If I walked further along the ridge I came to a house at the end of the path. After this point, the ridge disintegrated into a rocky slope that went down into the gully, and eventually reached the Tibetan quarter far below. Above was wild forest and in it dwelt truly wild animals.

The path continued in a very rough and intermittent manner down the length of the gully.

I had not yet had a chance to enjoy the privacy of my new dwelling, when my travelling companions from previously happened to walk by.

They saw me sitting on the balcony and greeted me with slow, lugubrious waves. They were feeling the effects of climbing the side of the valley while also being heavily stoned.

When they invited themselves in I felt obliged not to raise any objection, as that would have been really uncool. They settled themselves in, and lounged around the wood burning stove in the middle of the room. Then they began to make joints. These joints were made very differently to the ones that I constructed. These were produced by emptying a filter cigarette of its tobacco contents, and after heating some marijuana to cause it to be tender and crumbly, mixing it with the tobacco, and then gently, carefully refilling the empty cigarette.

Since in hippie philosophy there was no such things as personal possessions, it would have been a criminal act if I had claimed this cabin as my own private space. Therefore I could not ask these people to leave when they had overstayed their welcome. Because of this, I reluctantly accepted that I now had some fellow tenants, and that all hope of a quiet, stress free, reclusive life of meditation was, at least for now, shattered.

Joel, who had seemed to be their leader, soon made the place his own. They spoke in French a lot with little consideration for me, knowing that I was unable to understand them. The German guy Otto apparently spoke enough French to join them in conversation. I was too depressed most of the time to make the effort to bother speaking in German with Otto. Besides, like many Germans, he was taciturn, and considered idle chatter to be too trivial to merit his attention.

This group also seemed to have other business which in their opinion was far too serious and sensitive for me to be included. They were, as I have already mentioned, drug smugglers. I don't doubt that some of what they talked about was to do with how they were going to distribute and sell their wares.

There were no beds or bed frames in this cabin, only the packed earth floor. At night while I tried to get to sleep I could hear wild, or feral dogs. They came down from the forest above and fought over scraps from the nearby middens. Their yelping and yowling was not a pleasant sound at bedtime. It also meant that midnight strolls were certainly not a good idea.

In the mornings I would make my way down the gully to the Tibetan quarter of the town. I would then beg a few rupees from the wealthier looking Indians, usually Sikhs. Clearly they held me in contempt as a dirty Western hippie. But giving seemed to boost their own sense of righteousness, so in the end everyone went away happy. After acquiring some money I would amble down to the riverside shack that parodied as a café. Here I would slouch amongst a handful of customers who could be local, or they could be other Westerners. I would order a bowl of noodles swimming in an insipid meat soup of some kind. This seemed delicious to me at the time, as I had become used to a more meagre diet by now. The river doubled as a toilet for many of the locals, so there were a lot of flies padding around on the roughly cobbled together table at which I ate. Undoubtedly some of the flavour of the soup came from these disease festooned darklings. Dining there would have eventually sent people rushing down to the river for relief. Then the cycle of life would start all over again.

One day, on returning to the cabin I noticed a member of the group sitting cross-legged, stooped over, his attention focused on the inside crook of his elbow. In his left hand he held a syringe, and he was slowly, carefully moving the needle point towards a prominent vein in his arm. I didn't watch too closely, partly because of squeamishness, and partly because to be nonchalant was to be cool.

I sat down on the floor near the stove. Even though it was not cold, the stove in the centre of the room made a good focal point, and everybody looked towards it as they sat or lounged on the floor.

The person who had injected himself laid back with a look of relief and expectation on his face. Water was boiling on the stove for making *chai*. At times simple meals were made using rice, beans and vegetables. Chapatis could also be made on the flat top of the small stove. On the few occasions that we did have meals together a communal bowl was used, and each person would tear off a piece of chapati to dip out the next mouthful of food from the bowl. In the process fingers often came in contact with the food inside the communal bowl.

This was all part of the Eastern experience. We had said 'no' to the West, and this was how it was done out East. Death to the materialistic elegance of the knife, fork and spoon. Fingers were more natural. And of course this meant it was party time for every bacterium, virus and parasite in town. These parties always ended up as punch ups inside our delicate, lily white Westerner stomachs. So it was not surprising that I was malnourished by this point in my journey.

The flies were driving me mad as they crawled all over the multiple sores on my legs. I could not help but scratch myself, which only made the sores weep more, and so drew more flies. How it was that I did not end up with a really serious, life threatening disease, I do not know. It now seems like a miracle to me, and perhaps it was.

More and more frequently I was subjected to the unpleasant sight of someone shooting up drugs. I was still a long way from being willing to inject myself, but I did accept small amounts of opium that were given to me to take orally, as well as morphine powder that I snorted. The small black balls of opium seemed to have no effect on me at all; the same was true of the more refined morphine powder. This might have been a reflection of the level of depression I was suffering at the time.

There was a young man who was the same age as me and whose state of mind, like mine, involved a completely crushed personal confidence. My drug smuggling companions managed to recruit him into selling packets of drugs for them down in the town below. This meant that they did not have to take a direct risk themselves. They paid him a percentage from what he sold, but the amount was trivial considering the risks he was taking.

At the time, India was not a place in which you could expect to find justice. If you committed a crime, even a serious crime, and you had the money to pay a bribe, then you got off and you didn't need to suffer the consequences of your actions. However, if you were poor, then you were beaten up by the police, thrown into a prison that resembled a Dickens-style Victorian gaol, and the key would be tossed away with relish into some local latrine.

The young man only worked for these people for a short while, but he clearly did not realise the terrible risks he was taking.

Another potential way of making money, which also involved selling drugs but this time the softer, non-addictive drug marijuana, was 'rubbing'. For lovers of marijuana, India is a paradise. Marijuana plants grow everywhere, occupying the same ecological niche that nettles occupy in colder countries. If there was a piece of wasteland in a town or a village, then you could be sure there would be marijuana growing on it. It was such a natural sight that nobody, except newcomers, so much as blinked when walking past it. In the middle of Manali there was a large stand of marijuana plants, many of them over six feet tall.

It is incongruous to imagine hippies having a tough guy work ethic. But that is exactly what I saw there in Manali. Under the overbearing sun, their heads shielded by floppy brimmed hats that might have been bought from Aussies, were valiant looking hippies, their lithe silhouettes displayed against the blazing light, braving the heat and sweating substantially as they furiously rubbed their hands up the stems of the female marijuana plants. They were collecting the sticky resin onto their hands. When their hands were black enough, they would rub their palms together and then pack the secreted crumbs onto a growing ball. The end result was called *'charas'*, this was a high quality, highly valued form of marijuana.

When I tried rubbing I found that I became easily exhausted. This was due to the altitude, and to my depleted health. I could not help having admiration for the stamina of those who would work these plants for hours each day.

Also very unhippie-like was their motivation, which was for money. They would take the *charas* south to Goa and sell it at a price befitting its quality. Marijuana was illegal in India, but it was largely ignored by the police. A lot of small Himalayan farmers made their living in the same way as the hippies. Their fields were often remote and difficult to get to. Despite this they did occasionally have their crops destroyed by the authorities. However marijuana was impossible to control, or to monitor, because of its prevalence and its indigenous nature.

At this point in my life the notion of a God who was a person seemed like foolishness to me. Though the idea that a person could become 'God' did not seem ridiculous to me. The latter seemed in step with my beliefs in the currents, and laws, and principles, of an impersonal universe. In my thinking, persons who were ascended yogis transmitted messages of guidance to those who were spiritually attuned enough to hear them. What I didn't realise, was that at that time I was believing a perverse and twisted form of the truth. My opinion was that belief in God as a person that one prayed to, and who could hear prayers, was for little old ladies, children and silly people.

The idea of a relatively simple, impersonal spiritual machine seemed a lot more scientific to me. I can now see why a religion like Buddhism is favoured by many who call themselves scientifically minded. They think of everything in terms of 'Occam's Razor'. Which says that the simplest explanation for any problem or mystery is likely to be the correct one.

The truth is, my stubborn pride was blocking me from believing in God. Especially a kind and forgiving God, but one who also held people responsible for their actions. It was much easier to believe that none of what I was, or did, was my fault. It was much easier to believe in an amoral form of religion, such as Buddhism, which incorporates sin and violence as part of what it would call a natural and balanced universal principle.

I was however at my wits' end. I had not achieved Nirvana or even managed to climb a little higher on the spiritual ladder. In fact I sensed that I had slipped even lower down on any ladder that had any true meaning or significance when it came to life and living.

One day I was sitting outside a hippie run *chai* shop. I was lounging sullenly on a chair that had been placed on the opposite side of the small road. It was one of a row of chairs, each of which was occupied by a Westerner, most of whom looked as burnt out as me, and were probably having trouble with disease, altitude and heat in the same way I was.

Casually the person next to me passed me a small booklet, little more than a tract. It contained well drawn black and white cartoon work. The cartoonist was obviously going for realism rather than exaggeration or comedy.

The speech bubbles made for easy reading. Even so, my concentration and attention span at this point in time were not good enough, except to pick up the gist of what the tract was all about. It contained the story of Jesus, and as such it triggered a memory from a couple of years previously. I remembered that God wanted to save me from my sins. This was something I had heard in a church service that a friend had taken me to when I was about seventeen years old.

All of a sudden I prayed in my heart that God would save me from my sins. This was a massive turnabout in my thinking. Previously I had not believed in a God who was a person. I had been too proud to ask God for His charity, and too licentious to admit that there was such a thing as sin.

I felt a momentary sense of relief, as if a burden had been lifted from me. I believe this was the point of my conversion, when it could be said that I was 'born again'. I did not have a full conscious understanding of the gospel message at this point, but I believe all the essential components were there in embryonic form. And that as such it was inevitable that I would recognise and love the gospel of Christ when it was preached to me more clearly in later years.

There was no follow up from anybody after I had read this tract. The person next to me had casually handed it to me, and now seemed disinterested. I did not seek or expect anyone to engage with me about the subject matter, so eventually I just strolled off. My mind was confused and depressed so I soon forgot about my prayer. I believe however that God's hand was on me in a special way from that point onwards.

Eventually I decided to leave Manali. I don't know why. I had spent about two months there and I was restless again. That is as clearly as I can define it.

I headed down the valley to a town called Mandi.

I recall one evening attempting to enter a temple by ascending some steep steps, in the hope of finding food and shelter. A man stood at the top of the steps and barred my way. He was showing me the heel of his hand. He was obviously indicating that I should not go any further. I remember climbing back down the steps feeling very dejected.

Another night I entered a village and climbed into a sort of hay pantry situated outside the front door of someone's house. In the morning the owner came out, presumably to feed the goat, and found a hippie in the hay. Luckily for me he had a sense of humour, and called his whole family out to laugh at me.

I got to Mandi at the end of the valley and I was intent on continuing my spiritual search by going up the adjacent valley to Daramsala, which was the home of the Dalai Lama, the head of the Tibetan branch of the Buddhist religion.

A young man I had previously met in Manali, who for some reason hadn't impressed me a lot, happened to be travelling on the same road, and when he saw me he came over to talk.

Somehow he managed to convince me that Daramsala was not the destination for me, and that I should take the other road. I did this, I crossed a bridge and carried on through the town of Mandi. I was heading south towards Simla and eventually Delhi, the capital of India.

After walking through Mandi I stuck my thumb out and began to hitch-hike again. I had only the flimsy clothes I was wearing, and a dirty blanket over my shoulder. I was depressed, filthy, diseased, tired, lonely, malnourished and had sores all over my legs.

It was in this condition that I prayed again. I said to myself, "Okay, I don't have any visible friends, so I will have an invisible friend in Jesus." This childlike, and some might say childish thought, was accompanied by an assurance that these things were real. Once again I had a sense that burdens had been lifted from me. I have to make the point that this feeling was not strong and was only short lived, but it differed from anything I had done or thought prior to beginning to believe in God.

Previously the kindness of Jesus had not appealed to my pride. I had wanted to score spiritual hero points and bask in personal glory, not beg undeserved bread from a forgiving Saviour.

Chapter 19

The Start or The End ?

I will end this part of my story here even though that is probably a bit abrupt. The reason being that things actually got a lot more difficult from then on and I don't want to depress anyone with a catalogue of my miseries. Suffice to say that now at the age of sixty-eight I still believe in the kindness and mercy of Jesus through his gospel. To me his deity is no less than a fact. What I mean is that I know it to be true as surely as I know the ground is under my feet. I feel similarly about my sinfulness and the sinfulness of others, though the empirical evidence for that is more abundant. As for Jesus' death on the cross, it glows with a radiance that does not emanate from any of the other religions, a love that loves sinners, free forgiveness. By contrast all the other religions require ritual or futile personal effort, they demand some way of making up to a god or God, or they insist on the climbing of a spiritual ladder to get a person to heaven. Christianity says that the just punishment due for sin has been suffered by Jesus, even though he never sinned. It says that justice itself has been satisfied and therefore a sinner who comes to Jesus need no longer fear the judgement of God.

Chapter 20

SO WHAT BECAME OF THE FAILED HIPPIE ?

27 Years Later

The Night Shift

I slammed the swinging door open a little too hard. The wind and cold rain followed me in, and then subsided as I sighed with relief. I had had to spend an additional few miserable seconds securing my bicycle with a combination lock, so that none of the clients could make off with it, and concuss themselves in an inevitably clumsy attempt to ride it.

Relief was replaced by apprehension when I heard Philip's manic laughter. While most care workers eventually managed to come to terms with this insane cacophony, no one ever became completely used to it.

Philip's laughter was that of the mad professor, the spoof lunatic, the psychopathic killer, the mass murderer, the snapped mind. And this was for real, it was not affected in any way.

I knew in my head that this was a sign Philip was unlikely to be troublesome that night – but in my heart? No way was this good.

I waved to Helen who had appeared at the end of the corridor to check on the noisy back door. Satisfied, she waved back.

I had arrived early with a view to taking a shower after my nine mile cycle ride along the estuary path from Sandmouth. I viewed myself as fit, and enjoyed the wide eyed responses when I told people that I was in fact 47 years old. I had already gained a little kudos amongst the other staff for doing this ride in all weathers. This was another little bauble of pride that I could hang on the end of my finger. Tonight had been particularly rough, not just with the rain and wind, which were worse on the open estuary, but also with visibility. The driving rain and cloud cover had made it difficult to see where the estuary cycle track fell away into the water. My bicycle lights could not penetrate the constant relentless blast. In fact on one such night I had crashed into a fallen tree, luckily escaping with no more than a few scratches and bruises.

I was a now a little bit psyched up from the stress of my ride in the dark. This was not necessarily a bad thing if the night ahead was going to be a difficult one. I hoped not. I hoped I would be able to wind down now and enjoy a cuppa and a quiet chat with any residents who were still awake, and the other staff member who would be on shift with me. The chances of this actually happening were always about 50:50.

I went into the staff toilets to wash and change into dry clothes, after which I emerged bracing myself for what the night would throw at me. I didn't like to think too much about the 12 hours ahead of me, partly because there was no point. Whatever would be, would be. The previous shift were finishing their clients' bathing routines, and as much as possible they were getting them off to bed. However if someone had been hyper or problematic during the day, then bed was probably the last place they would be, and it would be my responsibility to contain and shepherd any trouble that might arise.

The background smells of the place registered with my nostrils as I walked along the corridor; my nose adjusted quickly to those now highly familiar three Ps - pee, poo and puke. These smells were the constant, irritating companions of all who worked in the main house. Any new staff always had to learn to swallow their bile and get used to these three little demons. Often the quality of their commitment was tested by how willing they were to put up with them.

I went to the staff office for the shift handover.

The first thing I did was to clock on. It had always seemed a bit incongruous to me to be clocking into such a people orientated job. In my mind you clocked on at factories, not at care homes. It felt to me like objectifying and depersonalising the people I was working with. Almost as if the clients were standardised cans in a factory, being pumped through a machine, rather than sentient individuals needing personalised care.

Nigel the day shift team leader was waiting for me.

Sonia, the female member of staff who would be working with me, was already there.

I gave Sonia a cursory nod, to which she responded in kind.

"How's things?" I asked Nigel.

"Philip's a bit hyper, but he's okay. Mary Trobello attempted to head butt Sheila several times today."

"Is she depressed?" I asked.

"We don't think so. She seems happy enough. We think she's just living up to her name, 'Mary Trouble'. Don't forget she has a reputation to keep."

"Derek is in his room, he was last checked half an hour ago. Quiet and compliant as usual. He's not likely to run off at night, but given his history with kids, don't let your guard down. Check him again at 9.30."

"I always do," I told him.

In fact it was the night staff's responsibility to check that all the clients in the house were present and correct at the beginning of their shift.

"Jeffrey hasn't had his medication yet, he refused it."

I groaned inwardly, my posture slumping somewhat. Refused medication always meant trouble, especially from someone as mentally confused as Jeffrey. I hoped this would be one of those rare occasions when it had been nothing more than a momentary mood blip.

I would leave that to Sonia though, since Jeffrey tended to respond better to females. As did most of the clients when they were feeling distress.

"Sam's had a good day at the farm," continued Nigel. "No doubt he will tell you all about it when you see him."

"Who's on the out units?" I asked.

"Roger Noland," replied Nigel.

Instantly I felt some relief. At least I had reliable back up if things went really bad.

In the main house there was only myself and Sonia responsible for 12 clients, all of whom were trouble in some form or another.

"Now if you don't mind, I'm off home to watch the football," insisted Nigel.

With that he handed me the pile of files containing the clients' daily records, grabbed his coat, twiddled his car keys, and made for the door.

"Who's on call?" I shouted just as Nigel was about to pull the door closed behind him.

"Samantha," came the reply just before the door clicked shut.

There was a quiet pause.

"He wasn't hanging about," commented Sonia.

"Do you think there's something he's not telling us?" I suggested.

She raised an eyebrow, as we both unconsciously took a deep breath and headed for the door.

We entered the clients' sitting room and stopped to look around. Ronald was sitting scrunched up on one of the deep window sills swinging his arm ape-like and glowering at us from under hooded eyes. Each time he swung his arm he would moan and say "Weng! Weng!" or something equally meaningless and inarticulate. He swung his arm a few times more before crying "Argh! – Stuart Thut – Argh!" and then moaning again he folded himself away, hiding his face. When Ronald swung his arm like that it usually meant he was offloading tension. And I was acutely aware that I might just have become a target for that very tension.

We left Ronald, because the worst thing to do when he was feeling stressed was to crowd him. You just had to leave him to it, and hope the inner pressure gradually bled way. The worrying thing about Ronald was that like some of the other clients, he had learnt to use anger as a form of stimulation, and he knew how to wind himself up into a frenzy, a bit like someone doing a war dance.

He was alone in the sitting room so there was no need to worry that he might suddenly lash out and punch somebody.

So Sonia and I went into the connecting lounge to see who was there.

Mary Trobello was with Sheila, her current day carer, who was obviously relieved to see us.

Sheila related how Mary had been an absolute little bitch today. To which Mary responded by tilting her head back and revealing a toothless smile. This was her way of laughing, silently. Mary was short, tubby and endearing, and it was difficult to believe that this smiling little ray of sunshine could possibly cause anyone any serious problems. But it was not idle humour that her name was sometimes mutated by staff to 'Mary

Trouble'. She had been responsible for least one broken jaw because of her habit of inflicting surprise head butts on people.

Despite this all the staff were very fond of her. She had a feistiness amid all the tragedy of her autism that was difficult not to admire.

She was at the severe end of the autistic spectrum.

Her more painful moments were when she looked in the mirror longing to be beautiful and seeing only a comedy staring back at her. At moments like that the pretty girls who stood next to her doing her hair were filled with sympathy, and found it easy to forgive the anger that sometimes lashed out at them, but usually plunged back down into Mary as self hatred and self harm.

Mary said something, the first part of which was lost, though the last part was clear: "--- fuckin' bitch". Her brow wrinkled when she said this but that expression was immediately replaced by one of her silent laughs.

"She's all yours," said Sheila and headed for the door, followed by a clumsy kick from Mary that didn't make contact.

"She's lying, fuckin' bitch is lying," said Mary in a voice that was relatively clear; this was unusual for her. Sonia ignored her.

"I wanna tea," said Mary in her high pitched mousy little voice, which just added to the illusion of innocence that surrounded her like a well set halo.

Sonia agreed to take her to the tea room. As they set off Mary, who was barefoot, did her characteristic hop and skip and then toddled along behind Sonia.

Apart from Ronald there was nobody else there. Then one of the door alarms went off and I rushed to the indicator board and pressed the cancel button. It was Peter. He was out of his room, probably to use the loo. I took the stairs at reasonable pace, two steps at a time but not rushing. Peter was rarely trouble and even when he did get stressed he was not violent. I got to the top of the stairs to find Peter outside his room fluttering his hands like butterflies and staring into them with rapt attention. When he saw me he hopped about in a way reminiscent of Mary and then headed for the toilet. Most of the clients were indiscreet when using the toilet so I checked that there were no females about while Peter did his pee. When he had finished he hopped once and returned to his room.

"Goodnight Peter," I said.

Peter made two rasping sounds before closing his door.

I sighed and listened to Ronald from the top of the stairs. Ronald sounded the same. He wasn't winding down, if anything he was getting worse.

I decided to do the room checks now. First stop was always Derek. I knocked on Derek's door. Derek opened his door just enough for me to see his head.

"How are you Derek?"

"I'm all right thank you Stuart," came the wheedling, subservient reply in the stretched out syllables of his strong Welsh accent. His head was held lower than mine and tilted round so that he looked up in a away can only be described as quintessentially creepy. His mouth was agape with an ingratiating smile. More than once Derek had unashamedly related his interest in little boys to staff. He seemed to make no attempt to hide who and what he was, almost as if he had made a kind of peace with it and was willing to live in this very restricted and controlled life without complaint. I didn't think any member of staff had let themselves be lulled into a false sense of security by this compliance. I certainly hadn't. Derek shut his door.

Next was Tina. Tina was tragically brain damaged. The care home had two young women who had suffered serious complications during childbirth. Tina was by far the most severely injured of the two, she could not talk and needed assistance to walk. She seemed to be trapped in a childhood zone somewhere close to that of a toddler. She was a cheerful soul and most of the women who worked with her found her to be a pleasure to look after. I knew she would be in bed by now, so I knocked on her door as a formality hoping that even to her simple state of mind this would convey respect.

I pushed the door slowly open and stuck my head round. The lights were off, apart from her bedside lamp which revealed a mewling lump of blankets that squirmed a bit.

I said "Goodnight Tina," to which she responded with more babyish mewling sounds and more small movements.

Satisfied that she was okay I closed the door slowly.

Mary's room was next door, but she was downstairs with Sonia so there was no need to check on her. I had already seen Peter tonight, so after listening for movement at his door and finding it quiet I moved on.

Philip was still cackling away. Probably sitting on the edge of his bed rocking. It was best not to disturb him because one never knew what might come out of him if he stopped to think. He was a well built, fit young man and even though he had a reputation for violent outbursts these had been mostly prior to my employment.

It is a strange recurring trait in many people with learning difficulties that they are also extremely strong. This can be unnerving for staff who sometimes have to deal with their distress when it manifests in very physical ways.

The truth was Philip frightened me and not without good reason. I had heard too many stories of Philip suddenly going berserk and setting off on smashing sprees, punching at walls and doors with fists like pile drivers followed up by powerful forearms propelled by formidable biceps.

The extra strength found in such people can often occur even when they look physically weak. The intensity of their tormented emotions can give a shivering skinny boy whose shorts look as if they are about to drop off him the strength to overpower strong men. This is no myth.

Philip, however, was already built like a young bull and full of energy.

Fit as I was, I knew I had no chance of stopping him or restraining him physically if he decided to go for it.

Philip could probably hear me doing my rounds but he seemed to be ignoring me.

I knocked on the door of one of the more able clients, Wally.

Wally represented a category of clients who were completely different from the severe autistics like Philip, Mary, Ronald and Peter.

Wally could articulate. And in conversation it sometimes took people who did not know him a little while before it became evident to them that he might have underlying mental difficulties. He was one of those people who at a pinch and with a bit of proper help would be capable of struggling along out in the community. His problems were mainly to do with psychological issues combined with low intelligence which meant he had trouble coping.

Wally opened his door.
"Hello Stuart."
"You okay?" I asked.
"Yeh! Fine. You?"
I answered him honestly. "Not bad."
I was never a bundle of joy at the start of the first shift of my seven nights of work. But I was up for the challenge, if it came.
"Can I come downstairs for a cuppa later?" asked Wally.
"Yes. of course. You don't have to ask," I replied .
Wally was a free agent in that his door alarm was always switched off. This was also true of all the clients of his level of ability, unless like Derek they represented a risk to others or to themselves.

After seven nights on I would then have seven days off. This was the shining star in the distance that made the subsequent shifts tolerable.
I continued my checks. I could tell it was going to be a long night.

✳✳✳

So that's what became of the failed hippie. He became a care worker looking after people with challenging behaviour. Not inappropriate considering.

✳✳✳

Thank you for reading my auto-novography. I would be grateful if you could post a review on Amazon and Goodreads. As an independent author your feedback is invaluable to me.

Printed in Great Britain
by Amazon